SOCIAL ROLES:

A FOCUS FOR SOCIAL STUDIES IN THE 1980S

By

Douglas P. Superka and Sharryl Hawke

A Project SPAN Report

Social Science Education Consortium, Inc.

Boulder, Colorado

1982

ORDERING INFORMATION

This book is available from:

SSEC Publications
855 Broadway
Boulder, Colorado 80302

ISBN 0-89994-274-1

Price: $9.95

Other Project SPAN Reports:

--Social Studies Reform: 1880-1980 (ISBN 0-89994-270-0; $12.95)

--The Current State of Social Studies: A Report of Project SPAN
    (ISBN 0-89994-272-5; $18.95)

--The Future of Social Studies: A Report and Summary of Project SPAN
    (ISBN 0-89994-273-3; $7.95)

--Working Papers from Project SPAN (ISBN 0-89994-275-X; $14.95)

Series Price: $49.50

This work was supported by the Research in Science Education (RISE)
Program of the National Science Foundation, Grant no. SED-7718598. Any
opinions, findings, and conclusions or recommendations expressed herein
are those of the authors and do not necessarily reflect the views of the
National Science Foundation.

Project SPAN undertook the task of describing and assessing the current and recent state of social studies/social science education, of designating desired states to which social studies might or should aspire, and of shaping recommendations as to how those desired states might be approached. This has been a formidable task, increasing in difficulty as the project moved from describing the current state to envisioning desired states to framing recommendations.

In describing the current state of social studies/social science education, the project began with three coordinated studies of science education supported by the National Science Foundation during the period 1976-78: a series of case studies conducted by the Center for Instructional Research and Curriculum Evaluation at the University of Illinois, a national survey conducted by the Research Triangle Institute, and a survey of literature for the period 1955-75, conducted by The Ohio State University with the assistance of the Social Science Education Consortium. These three studies, using three very different but congruent methodologies, provide a wealth of information about precollege education in natural science, mathematics, and social studies/social science education. In addition to these three fruitful sources, SPAN staff and consultants reviewed hundreds of other documents bearing on social studies and, through correspondence and at conferences, sought the advice and comments of many persons throughout the nation.

With respect to the specification of desired states and of recommendations for achieving them, the basic fact of social studies education at present is that there is a great diversity of opinion, from which it is impossible to elicit consensus. There are polar positions on the most basic issues, and a range of opinion between the poles. Some feel that social studies is in need of drastic revision, others that there is little or no need for concern.

The great diversity of opinion about desired states and recommendations that exists in the literature and in the opinions of social studies educators throughout the nation, as experienced by SPAN staff members in perusing the literature, in numerous meetings and conversations, and in voluminous correspondence, was also reflected in the twelve consultants who worked with the SPAN staff throughout the project. The twelve consultants were chosen for their known contributions to social studies literature and practice, also for their representation of various social studies roles: elementary or secondary teacher, consultant or supervisor at district or state level, professional association, university teacher. They were indeed "representative"--not only of social-studies-educator roles but also of a wide range of opinions about desired states and recommendations!

Given this diversity of opinion, both in the social studies field at large and within the group of consultants, the SPAN staff (within which there were also some differences of opinion!) had to take the ultimate responsibility for formulating the statements concerning desired states and recommendations. We wish to give full credit for information and ideas we have borrowed and used--borrowed both from the consultants and from social studies educators at large. But the staff must accept final responsibility for the content of the SPAN reports.

The staff members who worked with SPAN throughout the project are Irving Morrissett, Project Director and Executive Director of the Social Science Education Consortium, Douglas Superka, Associate Project Director and Staff Associate of SSEC, and Sharryl Hawke, Staff Associate of SSEC. Bruce Tipple, a Staff Associate of SSEC, also served as a staff member during the early part of the project, as did three Teacher Associates of SSEC, Maria Rydstedt, John Zola, and William Cleveland.

Two individuals produced commissioned papers at the request of the project staff. Dana Kurfman reviewed the status of evaluation processes in social studies and made recommendations on needed changes. Hazel Hertzberg wrote an extensive review of social studies reform efforts from 1880 to 1980.

The consultants who worked with SPAN throughout the project are:

Lee Anderson
Professor of Political Science
Northwestern University

Bob Beery
Social Studies Consultant
Rochester (Minnesota) Public
   Schools

Mary Vann Eslinger
Social Studies Consultant
North Carolina State Department
   of Education

Verna Fancett
Social Studies Teacher Emeritus
Fayetteville, NY

John D. Haas
Professor of Education
University of Colorado

James G. Lengel
Social Studies Consultant
Vermont State Department of
   Education

Jarrell McCracken
Teacher of Social Studies
Manual High School
Denver, CO

John U. Michaelis
Professor Emeritus of Education
University of California, Berkeley

Fred M. Newmann
Professor of Curriculum
   and Instruction
University of Wisconsin

John Patrick
Professor of Education
Indiana University

Elizabeth A. Pellett
Social Studies Consultant
Los Angeles County Schools

Roosevelt Ratliff
Associate Director for
   Affiliated Units
The Association for Supervision
   and Curriculum Development

This publication is one of a series of reports of Project SPAN.

FOREWORD

In the course of Project SPAN, consultants and staff wrestled with
the problem of whether a new content focus and a new curriculum organization pattern for K-12 social studies are desirable and/or feasible. As
described in the SPAN reports, the present pattern of topics and courses
has been in place for more than half a century. Modifications and devia-
tions of content and course titles have occurred, emphases have changed,
and new topics have been grafted onto the old structure--with varying
degrees of staying power--but the basic pattern of courses and topics
has remained quite stable.

Discussions addressed the two questions of desirability and feasibility of basic change in the dominant focus and course pattern of K-12
social studies. Opinions as to the desirability of basic change were
sharply divided. Some felt that the length of time that the dominant
organizational pattern has existed renders it suspect and that this
pattern has not accommodated and cannot accommodate new developments in
social knowledge, social needs, and student needs. Others felt that the
persistence of the old pattern is evidence of its usefulness and work-
ability rather than of obsolescence, that necessary changes can occur
and have occurred within the existing pattern, and that other aspects of
social studies education are more deserving of attention than efforts to
change the existing pattern.

Opinions with respect to the feasibility of change in the dominant
organizational pattern and the topics taught within the pattern were
less divided: there was general agreement that substantial changes in
the existing pattern in the near future are highly unlikely. The persistent pattern of textbooks and curriculum guides, as well as the experience and expectations of most social studies educators, tend to hold the
existing pattern rather firmly in place. Some, however, felt that a new
focus, such as concepts and skills, could be instituted within the existing course pattern.

Stimulated by such discussions and informed by their familiarity
with the extensive literature reviewed by Project SPAN, two staff members
struck out on their own to suggest an alternative focus for social
studies that might also involve a change in the dominant social studies

course pattern. In the four sections of this volume, Douglas Superka and Sharryl Hawke thoughtfully and thoroughly present a "social-roles" approach to social studies. While attention to social roles in social studies is not entirely new, as they point out, the elaboration of ideas and suggested applications presented by Superka and Hawke supply an unprecedented wealth of material for those who might wish to use social roles as the basis for a new approach to social studies.

Irving Morrissett

CONTENTS

PREFACE

Project SPAN has outlined six major problems which social studies educators need to address in the 1980s and a series of desired states and recommendations for improving social studies in the next decade. Since those are broad guidelines for improving the field, a number of different approaches to social studies could be advocated as the means of implementing those recommendations and achieving those desired states. This volume offers one possible focus for social studies that we believe can help in resolving the problems and achieving the desired states that have been described. This focus is called "social roles."

The first section of this publication, "A Perspective on Social Roles," describes the social-roles approach in detail. It is an expanded and revised version of an article which appeared in the November/December 1980 issue of Social Education. In this version, each of the social roles--citizen, worker, consumer, family member, friend, member of social groups, and self--is described, and the contribution of social studies to those roles is explained and illustrated. Also included are a justification for the approach and an explanation of how it can help alleviate the six problems and achieve the desired states identified by Project SPAN. This section concludes with a brief summary of other curriculum orientations similar to the social-roles approach and answers to several questions concerning the implications of this approach for the present social studies curriculum.

The second section, "Using Social Roles to Organize K-12 Social Studies," shows how this framework might be used as the basis for a K-12 curriculum. The section begins with a brief explanation of the importance of curriculum organization in improving social studies. This is followed by a description and illustration of a new way to organize elementary (K-6) social studies, based on the social roles. Possible curriculum implications for secondary social studies are then explained and illustrated. A brief summary of the advantages of a social-roles approach for K-12 social studies concludes this section.

"Social Roles: The Main Ideas" presents a succinct, point-by-point description of the main ideas related to each of the seven social roles. Listed for each role are ten or more main ideas that could be emphasized in the social studies curriculum; these ideas are drawn from a variety of sources in education and the social sciences. This list constitutes the initial step in identification of the conceptual substance of a social-roles curriculum.

The publication concludes with "Social Roles: Relating the Main Ideas to Topics and Courses," which illustrates how social roles can be used as a basis for refocusing existing secondary social studies courses. We have identified topics and courses in which each of the main ideas for the social roles can be effectively taught without completely revising the scope and sequence of high school social studies.

One very important point about the nature and purpose of this publication and our work on social roles needs to be clarified. The social-roles focus has been only a small part of our work on Project SPAN. It has never been our intention, nor did we have the time in the context of this project, to develop a complete curriculum for teaching social roles in social studies. Indeed, the initial purpose of our work was to stimulate the SPAN staff and consultants to think about possible recommendations for improving social studies in more concrete terms. Later, in writing the Social Education article, we hoped that the social-roles idea would stimulate reactions and ideas within the entire social studies profession. Many reactions, indeed, have resulted--both positive and negative. This volume, which contains the background papers we wrote to stimulate those reactions, is therefore not intended as a complete social studies curriculum that teachers can take and use in their classrooms. We hope, however, that the ideas and suggestions in this volume will help those teachers and other educators who would like to focus more social studies instruction on social roles to get started in that effort.

Douglas P. Superka
Sharryl Hawke
January 1982

A PERSPECTIVE ON SOCIAL ROLES

Seven Social Roles

How can social studies contribute more fully to the development of
informed and effective participants in our society? One way would be to
focus content and instruction more directly on how most people participate in that society--how they spend their time, where they put their
energy. Most people's social lives can be described by seven major
roles: citizen, worker, consumer, family member, friend, member of
various social groups, and self. Social studies can help young people
understand, value, and function creatively and competently in these
social roles--thereby helping them become effective individuals and
effective participants in our society.

The term "role" has been defined by sociologists and psychologists
in various ways. There is general agreement that the term refers to a
set of organized meanings and values that direct a person's actions in a
given situation or in the performance of a given function (Kitchens and
Muessig 1980, p. 11; Rose 1965, p. 45). Most anthropologists and sociologists add that these roles are usually ascribed to people by their
society or culture. Some emphasize that this process is interactive and
that individuals can exercise choice in defining and implementing their
roles within the society (e.g., Blumer 1970). Here the term "role" is
used in roughly this manner, placing particular attention on the situations (especially sets of relationships) and functions implied by a role.

Each of the seven roles defines an important area of social life in
which nearly all persons participate and implies a specific set of relationships and functions. As citizens we participate in various ways and
at several levels in the political (governmental and public policy)
aspects of society. The roles of consumer and worker define our essential relationships and functions in the marketplace and workplace,
respectively. The two major areas of close interpersonal relationships
are defined in our roles as family members and friends. We are also
members of various social groups, among them racial groups, ethnic
groups, gender (male-female) groups, age (child, adolescent, adult)
groups, religious groups, and socioeconomic classes. Our identifications

and relationships with the latter groups can have a significant influence on the previous five roles and on the last role--self. We use the term "self" broadly to define the role which consists primarily of our relationships to ourselves. The main function of self is the clarification and development of identity. This role is at the core of all the other social roles, but it also involves something beyond these roles.

While each role defines a distinct set of relationships and functions, all seven are interrelated. A method of illustrating the interrelationships between and among the seven social roles is depicted in Figure 1. Being a member of a labor union, for example, is part of a worker role; but it can also involve citizenship activities, since unions attempt to influence public policy. Many consumer functions occur within the context of the family. Social studies programs can highlight both the distinctiveness of and the interrelationships among the seven social roles.

Figure 1
THE SEVEN SOCIAL ROLES

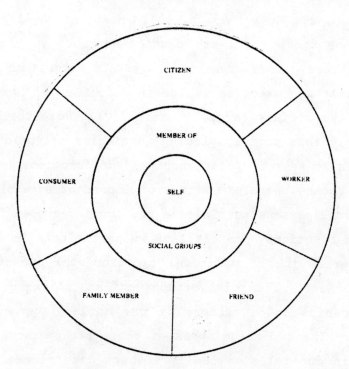

The social roles also have both individual and collective dimensions. As citizens, for example, we perform individual civic actions, such as voting in elections, but may also be members of local community groups or political parties that involve collective responsibilities and actions. Social studies can contribute to learning related to both of these vital dimensions.

To explain and illustrate the nature of these social roles and their interrelationships is the main purpose of this paper. A second purpose is to clarify the valuable contributions that social studies can make to education for the social roles. These social roles can serve as a useful framework for determining what to teach in social studies and why. In addition, social roles, in combination with knowledge about student development, can provide a concrete basis for organizing curriculum content and learning activities in social studies.

Citizen

Citizenship education has been considered the central goal of social studies for at least the past century (Hertzberg 1981). Moreover, within the context of the recent resurgence of interest in the topic, citizenship has been called the "primary, overriding purpose" (Barr, Barth, and Shermis 1977, pp. 67-68), the "centering concept" (Shaver 1977, p. 115), and the "ultimate justification" (Remy 1978b, p. 41) of social studies. The revised NCSS curriculum guidelines, state frameworks, district curriculum guides, and textbooks reflect this orientation.

Despite widespread agreement about its centrality and importance to social studies, however, there is little agreement about the meaning of citizenship, the nature and scope of the citizen role, or the major focus of citizenship education efforts (Meyer 1979, pp. 11-19). Each of the following ideas has been suggested as the central focus of citizenship education: knowledge from the social science disciplines (Berelson 1962, pp. 6-7); the knowledge, abilities, duties, freedoms, and ideals of a democratic citizen (Martin 1980, p. 285); commitment to democratic values (Butts 1979); analysis of public issues (Oliver and Shaver 1966); decision making (Remy 1976); moral reasoning (Fenton 1977); understanding global perspectives (Mendlovitz, Metcalf, and Washburn 1977); competence in group governance (Turner 1980); "just relations between individuals and social institutions" (Foshay and Burton 1976, p. 4); and influencing public policy (Newmann 1975). While some educators have stressed patriotism and loyalty, others have emphasized problem solving and social criticism. Some definitions of citizenship encompass nearly all areas of social life, while others are restricted to the political arena. Nearly everyone, however, agrees that the development of responsible participating citizens is a key to preserving and improving our democratic society.

The citizen role as defined in this paper is focused on the relationships between individuals and political entities (for example, the state, governmental agencies, and political organizations) and organized efforts to influence public policy. On the basis of this conception, the citizen role includes a wide range of important activities: voting, obeying just laws, challenging unjust laws, paying taxes, serving in the armed forces, participating in political parties, studying public issues, advocating positions on public policy questions (either individually or in groups), working for volunteer organizations, and holding public office. Citizens engage in these activities in a variety of settings and at several levels, including the neighborhood, community, city, state, region, nation, and world, with the specific nature of the citizen activities differing at the different levels.* Many of the activities performed at the city, state, and national levels are directly related to governmental institutions, while those at the neighborhood, region, and world levels are not.

Another useful distinction can be made concerning citizen activities at these various levels. Newmann (1980) has distinguished between "societal" level participation aimed at influencing elites who run large-scale institutions and "communal" level participation which involves small, face-to-face groups making self-governing decisions. Haas (1980) makes a similar distinction between efforts which develop societal commitment (gesellschaft) and those which foster communal feelings (gemeinschaft).

---

*Many other activities often considered in broad definitions of citizenship, we have defined in relation to the other social roles. Parents and children deciding where to go on vacation, for example, is considered under the role of family member.

In relation to all levels of the citizen role, social studies has a major and unique contribution to make. Although other subject areas and aspects of school share some responsibility for citizen education, social studies is primarily responsible for providing opportunities for students to learn the basic knowledge, skills, and values needed to understand and participate effectively in the U.S. political system and to analyze and help resolve public issues.

Exactly what is meant by education for the citizen role? Within history, political science, economics, and other subject disciplines, educators cannot only identify topics or concepts related to the citizen role but also determine which of these are most directly related to or essential to that role. Since history still occupies a major place in the social studies curriculum, questions need to be addressed concerning the contributions of history to the role of citizen as well as other roles. At the classroom level, for example, a high school teacher may have to decide what aspects of the "Civil War and Reconstruction" are most important for senior high students to learn in order to be informed citizens. At the district level, administrators might need to decide whether U.S. history is the best course for ten-year-olds.

Such questions do not mean that history should be considered unimportant. It does mean that history and the other disciplines should be examined to determine what knowledge and skills can contribute most to education for citizenship. These kinds of decisions will have to be made if room is to be found in the increasingly crowded social studies curriculum for teaching about the other important social roles. Young people and adults spend more than 90 percent of their waking time in these other roles; social studies in the 1980s can make a bigger contribution to these aspects of their lives.

Worker

The worker role, unlike the citizen role, is not generally perceived by social studies educators as being central to their field. Although some educators have supported the "infusion" of career awareness into social studies instruction (for example, Taylor et al. 1977; National Council for the Social Studies 1975), many teachers have viewed career education as an encroachment on the legitimate domain of social studies.

5

Social studies educators cannot ignore the fact that productive work is one of the most important aspects of most people's lives. A consistent finding of the various secondary education commissions of the 1970s was that education had failed to establish a meaningful relationship between school and work in our society (National Task Force for High School Reform 1975; National Commission on the Reform of Secondary Education 1973; Panel on Youth, President's Science Advisory Committee 1974). Work is an important part of many students' lives, even before they leave high school; a recent study reported that "at some given time during the school year, about 50 percent of all high school juniors and seniors and about 30 percent of all 9th- and 10th-graders are employed" (Cole 1980, pp. 44-46). And, of course, most students will spend the majority of their adult lives as paid employees. Thus, the worker role has both immediate and future relevance to elementary and secondary students.

What can social studies' contribution be to this role? Social studies has an auxiliary, not primary, responsibility in this area. The major responsibility must and should rest with career education specialists, guidance counselors, language arts, and mathematics teachers. These areas are proper ones to focus on the knowledge about careers and on occupation-related skills such as identifying information related to job openings, preparing job applications, interviewing for jobs, and performing basic computation and communication skills. Social studies can reinforce these efforts. Social studies also shares with other areas of school and society some responsibility for developing decision-making skills and constructive attitudes toward work.

In addition to these shared responsibilities, social studies can fulfill the following special functions: to provide students with awareness of careers directly related to the social sciences (e.g., urban planner, sociologist, government administrator, and business economist); to help students reflect on their worker-related experiences (e.g., analyzing interpersonal relationships and conflicts on the job); to provide students with knowledge that will place in historical and social perspective the role of the worker in U.S. society and the world (e.g., knowledge about labor unions, immigration and employment, women in the labor force, and the impact of war on jobs); to help students analyze

6

and discuss the interrelationships between the worker role and the other social roles (e.g., the conflicts that often arise between being a responsible member of the family and a conscientious worker).

Drawing on valid knowledge from economics, history, sociology, and other social sciences, social studies can make an important contribution to education related to the role of the worker.

Consumer

While not all people are workers or active citizens, everyone in our society is a consumer. The role of consumer is to buy and use the goods and services produced by workers. Defined broadly, these goods and services include natural resources (e.g., water, wood, oil, and gas), manufactured products (e.g., food, drugs, bicycles, and cars), information (including print and other media), business services (e.g., banking, insurance, and real estate), and social services (e.g., education, medicine, recreation, and welfare). The consumer role includes being a good planner, shopper, and protector of these goods and services and an effective money manager. Being a wise and competent consumer in our modern complex society will continue to be a major challenge in the 1980s and beyond.

The consumer role is sometimes perceived as an economic activity in which persons engage solely for their own individual benefit. The problems related to using energy and other environmental resources have demonstrated that the consumer role also has significant collective and societal dimensions. Buying a small car instead of a large one, for example, may be a long-term money saver for an individual. It may also be a more environmentally sound and socially responsible decision. Remy correctly points out that if this decision were consistent with our national energy policy, then the individual action of buying a car would be very much related to the citizen role as well (Remy 1978a, p. 13).

While consumer education has received renewed attention in the 1970s, its relation to social studies is not clear or well established (Remy 1978a). Social studies' major contribution to the role of consumer can be to help students understand this role in the context of our national economic, political, and social systems and to appreciate the global interdependence of consumers.

7

Meeting these goals suggests such topics as consumer law, supply and demand, consumer protection, inflation, money and credit, boycotts, energy, the environment, multinational corporations, and international trade. It also calls for teaching about interrelationships between the consumer and the other social roles.

Providing historical, economic, and political perspectives for the consumer role is another unique function of social studies. The emphasis should be on supplying students with conceptual tools they can use to adapt to future changes rather than providing technical skills that may be obsolete in ten years. A tennis instructor can help students make a wise decision about which tennis racquet to buy. A driver's education instructor can teach students what to look for in buying a car. A home economics teacher can help students become aware of the advantages and disadvantages of generic groceries. While social studies can make some contributions at that level, it should focus primarily on providing the larger view.

Social studies shares with other subject areas responsibility for some aspects of consumer education. Critical television viewing, for example, is a topic of interest in both social studies and language arts. As language arts concentrates on analyzing programs for literary quality and program elements, social studies can help students detect bias and stereotyping in both programming and advertisements by drawing on knowledge and skills from psychology and social psychology. Similarly, social studies and science share responsibility for helping students function effectively and intelligently as consumers of natural resources, especially in regard to such science-related issues as energy, acid rain, and recombinant DNA. The partnership between social studies and other subject areas in preparing students for the consumer role can be one of the most vital developments of the 1980s.

Family Member

Most demographers predict that the 1980s will not be an easy, stable time for families in the United States. Divorce rates will probably continue to rise, birth rates will remain low, more women will join the paid labor force, more children will live with only one parent, and more couples will decide not to have children. Despite these stresses, strains, and changes, most experts believe that the American family will adapt and survive. Because of these stresses, strains, and changes, young people will need all the help they can get to understand and function in their roles as family members.

Traditionally, the family has been defined as a group of people related by birth, marriage, or adoption who live together for the primary purposes of procreation and child rearing. It can also include alternative family styles—for example, a married couple living together without children—and such extended-family relationships as those between emancipated adults and their elderly parents. Family roles include mother, father, husband, wife, son, daughter, brother, and sister; also grandchild, grandparent, mother-in-law, and still others. Everyone functions in two or more family roles, often in two or more simultaneously. The nature of each of these roles changes dramatically over the course of a person's life. Societal trends add another element of change.

Social studies programs can and should make an important contribution to helping young people understand and function in their present and future roles as family members. Obviously, social studies cannot and should not be totally responsible for producing "good family members"; a young person's own family will certainly be the major influence. However, by drawing on knowledge from sociology, psychology, anthropology, and history, social studies can help students better understand and deal with parent-child relationships, sibling relationships, the rights and responsibilities of parents and children, changing family roles, the family as an institution, the future of the family, the diverse types of families in the United States and throughout the world, and marriage and courtship.

At present, the family is a specific focus of social studies only in the primary grades (especially grade 1) and in the 12th grade, as part of a sociology or family life elective; in other grades it is virtually ignored, despite the importance of family to the lives of early adolescents. The role of family member should have a more prominent place in K-12 social studies programs.

Friend

No social studies teacher, especially at the junior and senior high levels, has to be reminded that "friends" are one of the most important dimensions of students' lives. Compared to friends, social studies or any other subject area is far down on students' lists of interests, as a reading of the CSSE case studies confirms (Stake and Easley 1978). A recent study of teenage sexuality confirmed the importance of friendships in the lives of 15- to 18-year-olds ("Sex Rated Below Friends, School, and Sports" 1979).

Younger students also value friendship, but they think about it differently. According to research conducted by Robert L. Selman and Anne P. Selman, children's thinking about friendship develops in stages in much the same way as their reasoning about moral issues and other interpersonal relationships (Selman and Selman 1979). The Selmans also found that many youngsters need help in making and keeping friends and in dealing with friendship-related conflicts.

The importance of friends does not appear to diminish as one grows into adulthood, although the nature, forms, and bases of friendship change dramatically. While we lack extensive research data on friendship, such popular-culture indices as television shows ("Laverne and Shirley") and singles-club memberships suggest the importance of friendship in our society. The few studies which do exist (e.g., Block 1980 and Parlee 1979) confirm that the experience of friendship is crucial to the healthy social and emotional development of children and adults. Strained family relationships and alienation from the community underline the importance of friends as a source of trust, understanding, affection, and acceptance.

In contrast to the centrality of friendship in people's lives, the topic is virtually nonexistent in social studies. A few primary-level textbooks touch on the subject and some supplementary materials contain activities related to friendship. Of all the social roles, however, that of friend receives by far the least emphasis in social studies.

Social studies (along with language arts and counseling) has an important and legitimate contribution to make in this area. While a new educational movement (such as "Education for Responsible Friendship" or "Friend Education") is not being suggested here, there are some vital aspects of friendship that can be a part of schooling and social studies. Many students at all levels will respond to opportunities to examine and discuss questions related to friendship, and the social sciences have important knowledge and skills to offer in educating students for the role of friend. Appropriate topics include forms of friendship, ranging from casual to intimate, responsibilities and expectations associated with friendship, qualities of good friends, processes of making friends, social mobility, same-sex/opposite-sex friendships, conflicts between family and friends, peer groups, cross-cultural friendships, and wartime friendships.

Member of Social Groups

In addition to functioning in the other social roles, every person is also a member of various social groups. Broadly defined, these include (1) groups whose membership is determined at birth (being male or female, a member of a racial group, and a member of an age cohort group), (2) such categories as religious groups, ethnic groups, and socioeconomic classes, into which persons are born but from which they may move, and (3) groups to which people choose to belong, such as bridge clubs, baseball teams, and women's consciousness-raising groups.

Participation and membership in all these groups can take place at various levels of involvement; however, certain socially prescribed expectations and norms are associated with membership in each group. Social studies efforts in regard to membership in the first two kinds of groups should be focused on teaching students to be aware of the existence and nature of different kinds of groups, to analyze their particular affiliations with groups, to make conscious individual decisions about the extent of their participation in various groups, and to understand the nature and origins of group expectations--emphasizing that one does not necessarily have to limit his or her choices because of traditional group expectations. This has indeed been a major thrust of many multicultural education, ethnic studies, and women's equity efforts.

At the most intimate level, a person can choose to belong to a small face-to-face group whose primary goal is social or philosophical rather than political or whose organizing principle may be ethnic identity, religion, age, or sex. Some examples of groups in this category would be a social club based mainly on ethnic affiliation, a youth athletic club, a bridge club, and a local church or temple. A major contribution of social studies at this level can be to help students examine the nature, purpose, and dynamics of such groups--who belongs to these groups, where they exist, why they form, and how they are run--as well as group responsibilities, rules, and norms.

At still another level, a social group may be a large-scale (national or global) organization whose purpose is to help maintain and improve the social conditions of a particular group--for example, the National Organization for Women (NOW) and the National Association for the Advancement of Colored People (NAACP). The role of social studies in regard to such a group is to teach about its nature, purpose, function, and impact and to help students make reflective decisions about possible participation.

Still another type of group is a social aggregate lacking any kind of formal organization--males in the United States, children in the world, and Jews, for example. This category also includes members of geographically defined aggregates: people who live in the same river valley, mountain range, or desert, who have no political organization but share certain values and behavior because of their interaction with a common environment. Here the major role of social studies is to teach about the impact and contributions of such groups in the United States and the world--with attention to the groups' cultural traditions, customs, and history and the effects of major historical or contemporary forces on their social welfare. Examples of historical topics are the impact of the Civil War on blacks and the effect of economic recession and inflation on the roles of women in the United States. A very current topic related to these issues is the recent immigration to the United States of Cambodian refugees, Cubans, and other groups, resulting from international political events. The impact of this immigration on the United States and on these people is a very significant topic that social studies can teach.

Finally, social studies can contribute to students' understanding of the group-member role by focusing on the interrelationships between this role and the other social roles. Family roles, for example, are closely related to membership in ethnic groups. Another crucial topic is the potential conflict between the citizen role and membership in these social groups. Recent multicultural education efforts have helped to emphasize the pluralistic nature of our society and therefore of citizenship in the United States. Some, however, view this as fragmentation of the society and subordination of national civic values to ethnic and cultural values. The possible interrelationships between the citizen role and religious group member role have been dramatized by the direct involvement of some religious groups in recent political campaigns. Teaching directly and honestly about these kinds of conflicts and interrelationships today and in the past is a significant responsibility of social studies.

Self

As indicated in the previous discussion of social roles, U.S. society expects a person to be a good citizen, worker, consumer, family member, and to a lesser extent a good friend. In addition, our society often conveys certain expected ways a person should act based on the sex cohort role, ethnic group, and social class to which he or she belongs. Our society places still another expectation on people because of the high value it puts on the individual: people are also encouraged to be themselves—to express their own uniqueness and to develop their full potentialities. This striving for fulfillment and realization as a unique person occurs both within the six social roles (e.g., by being a unique teacher or the best father you can possibly be) and outside those roles (e.g., by reading history to expand your intellectual horizons or running ten miles a day to develop and maintain a healthy body). We have defined this function and the sets of relationships, meanings, and values associated with it as the role of self.*

---

*While it may not be common to use the term "self" as a "role," as it is used here, we believe this is convenient terminology for our present purpose, emphasizing the important relationship of the self to the "other" six social roles. This usage is similar to that of some sociologists and philosophers who have focused on an interactionist perspective on self and society (e.g., Bigge 1971; Blumer 1970). A similar view of the self role has also been taken by some social studies educators (e.g., Haas 1980).

The importance of including a focus on self has been recognized by many educators within and outside of the social studies field. Goals of increasing self-awareness and enhancing self-esteem have been a central aspect of humanistic education and values clarification (e.g., Canfield and Wells 1976; Raths, Harmin, and Simon 1978). Many social studies educators also include these goals (e.g., Fenton 1977).

As in the other roles, the role of self involves the person in certain kinds of activities. In addition to acting competently in the other roles, these self-development-oriented activities include developing a positive and realistic self-concept, increasing one's self-awareness, expanding one's intellectual capacities, developing and maintaining a healthy emotional and physical being, and clarifying and living by a set of personal values that leads to individual and societal well being.

All aspects of school and society share some responsibility for education and development related to the role of self. What is the unique contribution of social studies to this goal? It consists primarily of providing learning experiences that will help students understand how the other social roles, including membership in social groups, influence identity and self-development, as well as how the latter can influence and change social roles. To accomplish this goal social studies can draw on the social sciences--psychology, sociology, social psychology, history, anthropology, and cultural geography--as well as on such other sources as multicultural education, sex-role awareness, literature, and philosophy.

A final contribution of social studies and other subject areas to the goal of education for the role of self is to help each student expand and develop his or her intellectual capacity. This goal has two important aspects. One involves teaching content from social studies that students should know simply in order to be informed persons--even if such knowledge does not lead to immediate payoffs in terms of success in other social roles. The other is helping students develop a sense of the joy of learning and knowing. While much social studies knowledge can be justified on the basis that an informed person should know it, this should not be the sole focus of intellectual development. Social studies teachers need to strengthen ways in which they demonstrate to students that learning can be satisfying--even joyful--for its own sake.

Why Social Roles?

The goal of refocusing social studies on social roles cannot be easily attained, nor will it be a magical panacea for all of the problems of social studies. The social-roles focus is recommended in the belief that it will help, more than some existing approaches, to alleviate the six problems and move social studies toward the desired states recommended by Project SPAN. The basis for making this statement is explained below in relation to each problem area and desired state.

Student Learning

The most important problem to be addressed in the 1980s, and by implication the ultimate desired state to be achieved, is related to student learning and valuing of social studies. Since the study of social roles focuses on how children and adults spend time and act in the real social world, this orientation should help students appreciate the importance of social studies, increase student motivation to learn social studies, and, ultimately, improve students' learning of significant knowledge and skills in social studies. For most people, activities related to being a family member, worker, consumer, friend, and so on are very large and important parts of their social lives. The social-roles focus reflects this reality better than many recent social studies approaches. Citizenship approaches, reflecting either a cultural-continuity or a social-reconstruction orientation, place overwhelming emphasis on the citizen role--a role that is often defined primarily in terms of the political and public realm. Despite all the years of citizenship emphasis in social studies (Hertzberg 1981), few Americans today are active citizens and about one-third are politically indifferent (Marker 1980). Social studies educators should continue their efforts to change this situation, but should also be aware that most citizenship approaches tend to ignore or deemphasize other major social aspects of people's lives.

The social-science and reflective-inquiry approaches, while having more potential for stressing personal and other societal concerns, have also failed to provide a balance between the citizen role and other social roles. The former approach was more concerned with conveying the structure of the disciplines than with helping students relate and apply this knowledge in the real social world. Most manifestations of the latter approach tried to teach a generic process of scientific inquiry to deal with societal issues with little regard for students' developmental abilities and needs. These two approaches have demonstrated ability to attract the interest of a small minority of able, college-oriented students. The social roles approach, on the other hand, provides a focus that directly relates to most students' lives now and in the future. It, therefore, is more likely to stimulate broad student interest, motivation, and involvement in social studies.

While this hypothesis has not been tested empirically, one study which did relate to this idea is supportive. A study of 772 high school students' perceptions of the relationship of social studies to work, family, and community concluded that: "By developing the linkages of their subject matter to future personal development, (social studies) teachers could increase the likelihood that students would consider the subject important, and would work harder to learn it" (Farman, Natriello, and Dornbusch 1978, p. 38).

The social-roles focus can help students see the value of social studies. Can it also lead to increased learning of important social studies knowledge and skills? A case can be made for social roles having more potential to do that than some other approaches. First, the social roles provide a framework for asking: What knowledge and skills are most important for living in the social world? While there obviously is no easy way to answer this question, it is probably more pertinent than asking: What concepts and methodologies are most important to generate social science knowledge? What skills are needed to apply a general process of inquiry or decision making? or, What are the facts about U.S. history that all students should know? If helping students become effective participants in the social world is the ultimate goal of social studies, the social-roles focus might lead to a clarification of knowledge and skills that are more directly related to that goal and not entirely different from the knowledge and skills now being taught.

Second, social roles is more likely than other approaches to improve student learning because it has greater potential for stimulating student interest and motivation. A recent meta-analysis of educational research has demonstrated a consistent and positive relationship between student motivation and attitudes and student learning (Walberg, Schiller, and Haertel 1979). Common sense also suggests that students learn more when they are interested and involved in a subject and when they believe it is important and useful to them. Since the social-roles focus holds strong promise for increasing students' positive feelings toward social studies, it has real potential for improving student learning.

Third, a social-roles framework has great potential for using knowledge about student cognitive, moral, and social development that has been gained in the past decade or two. Unlike approaches that focus on one aspect of social studies (such as influencing public policy, learning basic facts and generalizations of a discipline, or being a responsible citizen), the social-roles approach with its balanced emphasis on personal, interpersonal, and societal issues will lend itself readily to integrating the implications of this important research.

A final point needs to be clarified concerning the relationship between the social-roles orientation and student needs and interest. A social-roles approach does not imply a total focus on student interest. High student interest is a necessary but not sufficient condition for good social studies. During the late sixties and early seventies, some social studies teachers made the interests of students the primary focus of their teaching, thus neglecting other important aspects of a social studies program. Some structure, such as that of the social roles, is needed to provide a stable focus within which student concerns can be considered. Without such a focus, an approach based solely on student concerns can be difficult to plan, can lead to much repetition, and can reinforce students' self-centeredness. The roles structure, on the other hand, can encourage students to see the connections among individual persons, groups of people, and social institutions. The roles focus can thus help students move beyond their egocentric orientations.

Teaching Practices

The central problem related to instruction that Project SPAN has identified is that most teachers do not use a variety of instructional practices in social studies, despite the fact that most educators believe that this should be done. Previous reform efforts have failed to change this situation, for a number of reasons. The inquiry movement of the 1960s tried to push one instructional strategy, which most teachers found difficult to implement and from which many students found it difficult to learn. Approaches that stressed primarily community-based activities encountered similar barriers, plus additional ones related to efforts to arrange for considerable out-of-school learning. A social roles focus, on the other hand, does not rely on any single instructional strategy. Indeed, a variety of practices will be needed to reach the varied goals related to education for citizens, family members, consumers, workers, and so on.

A recent study indicates that social studies teachers support integrative approaches and materials that relate knowledge to their students' lives (Fontana 1980, pp. 70-73). The social-roles approach places a major emphasis on this factor, an additional advantage that many other reform efforts have not had.

Curriculum

The major problem with the social studies curriculum today, as identified by Project SPAN, is that it is not organized around or focused on personal and societal goals that help students become effective participants in the social world. The social-roles focus is designed to alleviate this problem by emphasizing the wide range of roles in which people engage—from mainly personal ones such as friend and family member to societal ones such as consumer and citizen. The social roles framework, moreover, provides an excellent way to integrate the many diverse topic areas such as legal education, multicultural studies, consumer education, and career education. The roles also provide an understandable framework for integrating knowledge from history and the social science disciplines and for explicating the major knowledge, skill, value, and participation goals of social studies, as illustrated in Figures 2 and 3.

The four types of goals listed in Figure 2 can be considered in relation to the social roles. The following questions, for example, can be asked when planning a social studies program: What knowledge and skills are most useful for helping students understand and function in their roles as members of the family? What values and participation goals are particularly relevant to the consumer and worker roles?

Figure 2

SOCIAL STUDIES GOALS AND SOCIAL ROLES

SOCIAL ROLES

TYPES OF GOALS:	CITIZEN	WORKER	CONSUMER	FAMILY	FRIEND	GROUPS	SELF
KNOWLEDGE							
Facts							
Concepts							
Generalizations							
Theories							
SKILLS							
Critical Thinking							
Communication							
Creative Thinking							
Decision Making							
Observation							
Interpersonal/ Group Process							
VALUING							
Analysis/ Clarification							
Moral Reasoning							
Modeling							
PARTICIPATION							
Study of Social Problems							
Social Action							

Figure 3

SOURCES OF KNOWLEDGE AND SOCIAL ROLES

DISCIPLINES	SOCIAL ROLES						
	CITIZEN	WORKER	CONSUMER	FAMILY	FRIEND	GROUPS	SELF
History							
Geography							
Political Science							
Economics							
Psychology							
Sociology							
Anthropology							
SPECIAL TOPICS							
Citizenship							
Consumer Ed.							
Career Ed.							
Legal Ed.							
Global Ed.							
Multicultural Studies							
Women's Studies							
Future Studies							
Aging & Death							
Energy and Environment							
Population							
Urban Studies							
Science-Related Social Issues							

Similar questions can be asked in relation to the social science disciplines and special topics listed in Figure 3. Some questions related to the disciplines are: What knowledge from sociology and psychology is especially important to help students understand family roles and friendship? What knowledge from economics is most useful in relation to the worker and consumer roles? What political science concepts and generalizations are most vital to helping students become better citizens? The focus can also be turned around to question traditional elements of social studies programs: To what role or roles do American history courses most contribute? World history courses? Psychology and sociology courses?

The same kinds of questions can be asked of the various special topics such as legal education, environmental education, global education, multicultural education, consumer education, career education, women's studies, and future studies. Most advocates of these special topics push for their inclusion in all courses. Thus, for example, proponents of global perspectives say it should be stressed in all courses--U.S. history, world history, civics, government, etc. Multicultural proponents want the same thing, as do the others. But teachers cannot do everything in every course. Some topics are more appropriate for certain goals than others. The roles can help social studies educators make these curriculum decisions.

The roles, then, have strong potential for developing a comprehensive social studies curriculum based on personal and societal issues. Moreover, the roles provide a curriculum focus that can integrate three previously competing perspectives of social studies--subject, learner, and society. Most approaches to social studies in the past have stressed one of these perspectives at the expense of the other two. Schneider defined this problem as "the general lack of coherent, systematic curricula that gave balanced attention to the social sciences, to the needs and interests of pupils, and to significant issues and trends" (Schneider 1980, p. 30). The social roles provide a focus for social studies that can provide a balanced approach to these three important factors. Actual implementation of the curriculum approach described here in a school, district, or state will, of course, depend upon many other factors, including the availability of materials, the ability to demonstrate that the intellectual integrity of the disciplines can be maintained, and the ability to convince the public that such a curriculum is needed and will not sacrifice important basics. The potential for crossing these barriers with the social-roles focus has great promise.

Profession

The SPAN problems and desired states related to the social studies profession point to several areas that need improving. A social-roles focus is consistent with the directions suggested for these areas and may be a better way to achieve some of those desired states than existing approaches to social studies.

One of the primary needs identified by Project SPAN for improving the profession is to develop a greater sense of unity of purpose and direction for social studies that can point the way toward increasing students' learning and valuing of social studies. One can argue that there already exists substantial agreement about the central purpose of social studies. At the classroom level, most teachers' behavior and instruction reflects the notion that learning the facts and generalizations of history, geography, and some other social sciences is the key purpose of social studies. This purpose has not, however, demonstrated much potential for increasing students' learning of important social studies knowledge. Indeed, it seems to have helped to turn students off to social studies. Therefore, this purpose does not appear to be a desirable one for social studies educators to rally around in the 1980s.

At a very general level, there is also considerable agreement within the profession that citizenship education is the main purpose of social studies. There is, however, extensive disagreement and conflict over what "citizenship education" means and what directions that education should take. Even if social studies educators could agree on these issues, we have already discussed why we believe "citizenship" is too limited a focus for social studies in the 1980s and beyond.

The clearest evidence of the lack of unity of purpose and direction in the profession, however, exists at the more theoretical levels. Morrissett and Haas discuss the various approaches and rationales for social studies and the different classification systems used to describe them that have been posited in the last 20 years. More often than not, these approaches (e.g., reflective inquiry, social science disciplines, citizenship transmission, and student-centered) have been considered as alternative directions for social studies (Morrissett and Haas 1982). The critical need now is to develop approaches to social studies that synthesize the best elements of each of these various perspectives and point toward helping students understand and act effectively in their social lives.

The social-roles focus is one such approach. The way in which this focus can provide a comprehensive and integrative framework for the social studies curriculum has been described above. In a similar way, the roles focus has considerable potential for providing a sense of unity and direction for the profession. The roles focus calls for providing learning experiences and for teaching knowledge, skills, and values that will help students understand and act effectively in the major roles in which they engage in the social world. This will require students to learn facts, concepts, and generalizations from history and the social science disciplines; it will involve developing reflective thinking and rational decision-making skills; and it will include developing some basic values and discussing value issues. But instead of doing these things without a clear purpose and instead of competing for attention, proponents of these approaches can see where and how each of their views fits into the overall purpose of social studies. The roles, therefore, can be an effective way to provide a greater sense of unity and direction to the profession.

Another major problem in the social studies profession identified by Project SPAN is the low level of constructive interaction among the various members of the profession. Many different things need to be done to improve this situation, as indicated by the SPAN reports. The social-roles focus is consistent with these recommendations. Moreover, efforts to establish a social-roles focus on a K-12 basis can encourage interaction among elementary, junior-high, and senior-high social studies teachers. This would, of course, be true for any attempt to provide a K-12 focus for social studies, but the roles, perhaps more than other approaches to social studies, can also provide a strong basis for fostering communication between social studies educators and other subject area teachers. As indicated in previous discussions of the roles, subjects like language arts, science, math, and guidance also have important contributions to make toward the education of citizens, consumers, workers, friends, and so on. Defining social studies as the social sciences simplified for pedagogical purposes or as citizenship education, on the other hand, does not encourage interaction with other subject areas.

A third aspect of the problem of the social studies profession that Project SPAN has defined is the lack of meaningful professional growth opportunities for social studies teachers. The SPAN desired states and recommendations point toward better preservice and inservice training for social studies teachers and more effective staff development and teacher renewal activities. A social-roles focus will not automatically achieve these important reforms but is consistent with such efforts. Moreover, it can provide the rationale and framework for those efforts. Many teachers will need help in order to implement a social-roles approach. This can be provided, for example, by practical workshops designed to demonstrate how new activities can be taught in U.S. history in order to emphasize the various social roles. If teachers want to focus on social roles, these kinds of inservice programs will be useful and meaningful to them. It is not likely that all social studies teachers will want to participate in such activities, and it is probably unwise to try to force the teaching of social roles. The experiences of the federally funded curriculum projects emphasizes that unless teachers see that new materials or instructional practices will satisfy their needs, there is little chance of change.

The final important problem of the profession identified by Project SPAN is the relatively low level of satisfaction among social studies teachers. Increasing the level of teacher satisfaction will not be easy and will require a wide range of activities, such as those discussed in the SPAN recommendations. Social roles is certainly no panacea for this problem. The roles, however, can contribute to its alleviation by providing teachers with a comprehensive and understandable statement of the central purpose of social studies and by providing a framework whereby teachers at all levels and of varying perspectives can contribute to achieving this purpose. Moreover, some teacher dissatisfaction is related to students' negative feelings toward social studies. Since the

roles have a strong potential for improving student involvement and
interest in social studies, this approach may help to improve teachers'
feelings toward their profession.

This connection between teacher and student satisfaction points to
another aspect of this problem. Social studies teachers (and students)
need to feel that they are doing something that is special and important.
Currently, neither group seems to have that feeling. Various factors
are responsible for this situation. One powerful factor is the emphasis
on basics--defined by most educators and most of the public as reading,
writing, and math. This emphasis especially affects social studies
teaching at the elementary levels, where those priorities are obvious in
the amount of time spent on instruction and in the expressed concerns of
parents. It is also true, however, at the secondary level, particularly
in districts with declining enrollments and shrinking budgets. Many
secondary social studies teachers have responded by trying to define
social studies as citizenship education and by trying to elevate citizenship as another basic. Others have argued that social studies is important because students need something to read and write about. These
efforts to raise the importance of social studies, however, seem to be
the result of defensiveness and political expediency. The importance of
social studies can and should be established on the basis of its inherent
value in helping people understand and act in the social world. The
social-roles focus emphasizes this point and can establish a more stable
basis for the importance of social studies. It can, therefore, be a
significant factor in increasing social studies teachers' feelings of
worth and satisfaction with the profession.

Culture of the School

A major problem which inhibited most of the social studies reform
efforts in the past two decades was ignorance of the dominant school
culture (Anderson 1982). The social-roles framework takes into account
this very powerful influence. The roles, in fact, are more consistent
with the complex culture of schools and the place of schools in today's
society than some other approaches. Social studies programs focusing on
active participatory democracy, for example, have always encountered
difficulty because schools are not based and run on democratic princi-

ples. Curricula that place great emphasis on schools as laboratories for democracy and on democracy as the prevailing practice in U.S. society are unrealistic. Authority, control, and socialization are important factors in the school, marketplace, workplace, and home. The social roles provide a framework that recognizes and uses the fact that schools and society have complex cultures, often with conflicting value orientations. Within this framework, attempts to foster participatory democracy have a place, as does recognition of the need to foster responsibility and respect for authority in the home and workplace.

Most schools will probably never be laboratories for democracy. Some aspects of schools may be appropriate for learning about democracy, while other aspects may more appropriately be settings to prepare students for their roles as workers, consumers, and friends. Thus, the roles framework, instead of clashing with the school culture, can be used to enhance social studies learning. In addition, the social roles provide a reason for modifying some negative aspects of the school culture such as the nearly total isolation of social studies teachers from other teachers.

The problems related to the culture of the school in U.S. society will not be solved by any one approach to social studies. The social-roles approach, however, is more sensitive to this factor than previous social studies approaches.

Public Awareness

The sixth problem identified by Project SPAN points to the need for more public awareness of, support for, and involvement in social studies in the 1980s. This will not be easily attained. As stated earlier, some educators have tried to attract public support by emphasizing social studies as education for responsible citizenship or as content for the basic skills. Others have returned to the "basics of social studies"-- history, government, and geography. These routes undoubtedly would provide the least resistance to obtaining widespread public support in the short run. However, they also take social studies away from its most compelling and inherently valuable purpose--to help students understand and act effectively in the social world. We believe that longer, more difficult routes to gaining public support and involvement for this kind of social studies will be worth the effort.

The adult public, according to a recent Gallup poll, shares students' belief that their social studies classes are not very useful and relevant to their lives (Gallup 1978). Paradoxically, they still rate U.S. history and government as essential subjects (Gallup 1979). Both views, however, are probably tied to the realities they experienced as students--those courses were required for them and they were not very relevant for them. Personal and societal relevancy is one important aspect of the social-roles approach. If social studies educators can demonstrate this to the public, a major step toward public understanding and support will be achieved.

Thus, efforts to educate the public must accompany efforts to gain involvement and support. The social roles have an important advantage over other social studies reform approaches in these efforts. The roles can be explained in simple, understandable terms--citizen, consumer, worker, friend, parent, child, and so on--to which the public can relate. Previous reform approaches had to overcome jargonistic terms such as "interdisciplinary social science concepts" and "reflective inquiry processes" when communicating with laypeople. This advantage will not guarantee support, but it will help maximize clear communication and minimize professional intimidation.

It is also important to recognize that the public (despite our use of this term) is not a monolithic, homogeneous group. The public really consists of many different groups of adults who are very pluralistic in backgrounds, experiences, and values. While public opinion polls reveal some majority opinions, they also reveal many differences. A recent Gallup poll, for instance, indicates that "the public" is roughly split in half over whether high schools should offer fewer courses or a wider variety of courses (Gallup 1979). If more differences such as this exist, some segments of the public may be very receptive to the social-roles focus. Some of this support would probably come from people who have liberal views on education. The roles focus, however, also has some potential for appealing to people with conservative views. Those who believe that productive work and a strong family are the bedrocks of American society, for example, may respond to the emphasis placed on the worker and family-member roles.

Similar Curriculum Orientations

The social-roles focus is not an entirely new idea in curriculum. While this specific conception is somewhat different from other formulations, it is related to the long tradition of educational reform efforts that stress education for learning how to live in society rather than merely learning a body of knowledge for its own sake.

The theme of social roles is similar to that of the 1918 "seven cardinal principles," which also reflected a more utilitarian orientation to education. Those principles included worthy home membership, vocation, citizenship, worthy use of leisure, and ethical character--principles directly related to several of our social roles.

The social-roles focus is also similar to the so-called "life-adjustment education" movement of the late 1940s and early 1950s. This movement also stemmed from a desire to develop educational programs that more directly met the needs of youth and of society. Contrary to the connotation of the title, advocates of this approach did not stress merely "adjustment to existing conditions," but emphasized "active and creative achievements" and "learning to make wise choices" (Tanner and Tanner 1975, p. 339). Their focus, like that of social roles, was not conformity but reality.

One proposal offered to implement the life-adjustment goal was a curriculum based on "persistent life situations" (Stratemeyer et al. 1947). This idea emphasized focusing on the immediate concerns (not superficial interests) of children in order to "develop constantly broadening insights and deepening generalizations about problems of significance to them" (Tanner and Tanner 1975, p. 340). Examples of recurring situations were suggested in relation to developmental stages of children, but no preplanned curriculum was offered. There are some similarities and differences between this idea and social roles. The similarities include a concern for the needs of youth that goes beyond superficial interests, a desire for the curriculum to be more related to real life, and an awareness of the importance of relating learning to developmental stages. There are, however, several key differences. The "life situations" idea is clearly child-centered, while our social-roles focus reflects more of a synthesis of child- and society-centered orientations. The social-roles focus, in addition, lends itself more readily to a preplanned curriculum that still allows for adaptation to the needs of particular teachers and groups of students. Stratemeyer and her associates, on the other hand, stressed "that the intrinsic motivation provided by specific concerns of individuals and groups will, in the long run, result in a more effective selection of learnings than will any preplanned structure" (Tanner and Tanner 1975, p. 341).

The social-roles idea is consistent with and similar to other, more recent approaches that stress life-coping skills, survival skills, and broad conceptions of "basic skills." NAEP, for example, has identified several categories of basic skills objectives related to the social roles. These include consumer skills, career and occupational skills, health maintenance skills, interpersonal skills, citizenship skills, and family planning skills (NAEP 1975). Similar skills have been used by Dufty (1980) in proposing "living skills as a core curriculum component." The state of Georgia adopted a set of "contemporary life role skills" as part of the high school graduation requirements in that state (High School Graduation Requirements 1976). These approaches, however, emphasize discrete skills, while the social-roles focus also places importance on knowledge and values.

The idea that perhaps is most closely related to our social roles conception is the "lifelong roles" proposed by Joyce and Alleman-Brooks as a new focus for elementary social studies (Joyce and Alleman-Brooks 1979). Our social-roles focus was developed and elaborated independently of the lifelong roles approach and with no prior knowledge of it. There are several obvious similarities. The five "lifelong" roles—citizenship, family membership, occupation, avocation, and personal efficacy—are somewhat parallel to the citizen, family member, worker, consumer, and self roles. Both approaches advocate that the primary purpose of social studies should be to help students become knowledgeable, effective, and active in these roles (Joyce and Alleman-Brooks 1979, p. 5). Both approaches include knowledge, skills, values, and participation goals. One major difference between the two ideas is that the social roles also include two additional roles—member of social groups and friend. The consumer role in our conception also includes more than avocation. These topics are dealt with by Joyce and Alleman-

29

Brooks by identifying ten "organizing themes" that include consumerism, ecology, energy, intercultural relations, human equality, and morality (Joyce and Alleman-Brooks 1979, p. 7), these themes to be developed with the lifelong roles. A final difference between the two proposals is that the lifelong roles are suggested only for elementary social studies, while we are recommending that social roles be a unifying focus for K-12 social studies. These differences aside, the two approaches share a common vision of a better social studies curriculum for the 1980s.

Some Questions and Answers About Social Roles

Some of the questions that might be raised about the focus on social roles suggested here, and possible answers to these questions, are discussed below.

Would adoption of social roles as an organizing focus mean virtual abandonment of the present social studies curriculum? No; much of the present content could be kept. Many existing courses, current activities, and available materials contain valuable elements for teaching social roles. Historical perspectives and concepts, for example, are valuable sources of knowledge to help people understand and function well as citizens, consumers, and family members, and so on, in our rapidly changing society.

Would adoption of social roles as a focus of social studies relegate citizenship to a minor role in the curriculum? No; citizenship could, and probably should, remain the single most important role in social studies. Citizenship would, however, give way to greater emphasis on the other roles. The shift in emphasis might be illustrated as in Figure 4. (The "current emphasis" in Figure 4 represents the rhetoric of social studies rather than the reality. While citizenship is widely proclaimed as the only or dominant goal of social studies, the reality is that much of social studies is unrelated to citizenship or to any other discernible goal. Social roles can furnish a focus that is now missing in much of social studies teaching.)

Figure 4

SUGGESTED CHANGE IN EMPHASIS

ON VARIOUS SOCIAL ROLES

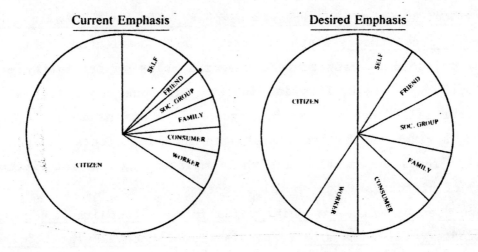

In a curriculum based on social roles, is there any place for topics based on social concerns which have come into the curriculum recently--such as multicultural studies, women's studies, future studies, and global issues? Yes; social roles can provide a useful framework for selecting and organizing subject matter related to these concerns. Studying families of different ethnic groups or in different cultures, for example, will not only enhance multicultural awareness but will help students place their own family roles and membership in ethnic groups in perspective. Focusing on the possible roles of consumers and workers in the 21st century can add additional relevance to future-studies programs.

Doesn't a focus on social roles imply that students are to be indoctrinated into passive acceptance of the roles assigned to them by society? No; using the roles as a focus and organizer for social studies instruction does not necessarily imply indoctrination. Like any other focus, the roles provide a setting within which students can and should deal with the interplay between individual goals and societal goals, social maintenance and social change, and self-actualization and socialization. Most of these social roles have changed dramatically in the past 20 years; more changes in the future are inevitable. Preparing students for these and other emerging roles in the future will mean much more than instilling a set of proper norms and behaviors.

Doesn't a social-roles emphasis suggest a low level of intellectual endeavor--a "Mickey Mouse" type of curriculum? As with any other goal or focus, it would be easy to reduce social roles to triviality--with courses such as "Your Friends in History" and "One Hundred Ways to Enhance your Self-Concept Through Geography." This need not happen. The examples given in the preceding pages should indicate that it is possible to focus on social roles while maintaining the intellectual integrity of history and the social sciences.

Doesn't an emphasis on social roles in social studies imply that social studies will bear sole responsibility for developing informed, competent, and committed citizens, workers, consumers, and so on? No; other subject areas and aspects of school life have important contributions to those roles. Science teachers, for example, share at least an equal responsibility with social studies teachers for helping students become wise consumers of energy and other environmental resources. Beyond the school, other social institutions (e.g., family, media, business, and church) have a powerful influence in social-roles development. A young person's own family, for instance, has an enormous impact on the kind of parent or spouse he or she will be. Social studies does, however, have a valuable contribution to make to education related to the social roles--within the school, probably the greatest contribution.

USING SOCIAL ROLES TO ORGANIZE K-12 SOCIAL STUDIES

Social Roles and Curriculum Organization

The seven social roles defined in the preceding section have important implications for all aspects of social studies education. Our focus
in this section is on the possible implications of social roles for
organizing a K-12 social studies curriculum.

Curriculum organization has been chosen as a focus for several
reasons. First, it is clear from the National Science Foundation data
that a standard curriculum pattern prevails throughout the country (Weiss
1978, pp. 49-66; Wiley 1977, pp. 37-39; Shaver, Davis, and Helburn 1979,
p. 24). This curriculum has been in wide use since the 1920s, held in
place not only by state laws and district mandates but also by textbook
programs, preservice teacher preparation, and tradition. Although this
organizational scheme has been challenged from time to time, few chal-
lenges have had significant impact (Schneider 1980; Joyce and Alleman-
Brooks 1979).

There is reason to believe that the prevailing K-12 organizational
scheme contributes to problems associated with student learning and
attitudes. For example, the fact that students in junior high school
have less-positive attitudes toward social studies than their elementary-
school counterparts (Wright 1980) may be due in part to the abrupt shift
from the more interdisciplinary, child-centered curriculum offered at
the elementary level to the discipline-structured geography and history
courses taught in junior high. More generally, the heavy concentration
of historical survey courses and place geography in most K-12 curricula
may contribute to students' perceptions of social studies as being
irrelevant and uninteresting (Stake and Easley 1978, pp. 13: 26-31).
Course structures that emphasize the presentation of factual information
may help account for the finding that secondary students develop facility
in recalling low-level facts but relatively less facility in applying
knowledge to solving problems (NAEP 1978, pp. 8-9).

Similarly, the predominant curriculum pattern may contribute to the
relatively high level of dissatisfaction expressed by social studies
teachers in comparison to teachers in other disciplines (Wright 1979).

One source of teacher dissatisfaction is lack of certainty about the ultimate aims of social studies education--an uncertainty that seems heightened by a K-12 organizational scheme in which the elementary curriculum bears little resemblance to or continuity with the secondary curriculum, in which U.S. history is repeated three or more times with little variation of goals or approaches, and in which subject matter is taught in a sequence that seems unrelated to students' needs, abilities, and interests.

Therefore, a focus on curriculum organization may provide a key to social studies improvement on both a local and national basis. While making changes in content will not automatically improve instructional practices or student learning, we believe that most teachers are more interested in "what to teach at my grade level" than in rationales or instructional theories. Changing what is taught may help initiate instructional changes that could lead to improved student learning and attitudes and increased teacher satisfaction.

This paper deals only with topical content. The following sections focus on generalizations related to the social roles, but a framework of skills and values related to the social roles has not yet been developed. Moreover, the organizational scheme suggested in this and the following sections will provide only a broad framework of what to teach at various grade levels. The specifics of which topics to place at which grade levels need to be developed with careful attention to recent research summaries on student development, such as those done by Torney (1980) and Martorella (1979). (For a provocative discussion of the caution which needs to be exercised in applying developmental research to curriculum prescriptions, see Shaver 1979.) Such work is not within the scope of the SPAN project and must await the efforts of future developers.

The curriculum reorganization plan suggested below shows how a social-role focus can be helpful in deciding what to teach and how to arrange course content. It is intended to be illustrative and represents one possible reorganization based on social roles. It is presented as a rather "pure" application of social roles; the reader is invited to consider modifications or partial uses.

34

Social Roles in the K-6 Curriculum

Since the 1920s, the expanding environments concept of K-6 social studies curriculum organization has made geographic place the central organizer at each grade level--for example, home/family in grade 1, school in grade 2, and community in grade 3. Were social roles used to organize the elementary curriculum, "place" would be removed as the central organizer and social roles would be substituted. All seven roles would be taught each year in a repeated, spiral sequence. In grade 1 students would learn certain kinds of knowledge about the seven roles, develop certain skills relevant to the roles, and consider values and attitudes related to the roles. In grade 2, students would again consider each role, but the second-grade curriculum would cover different topics, present new or more-sophisticated skills, and consider new or more-complex value issues.

The matrix in Figure 5 provides examples of topics arranged by social roles in a K-6 curriculum. By reading down each column, the variety of topics from grade to grade can be seen. Note that within the broad framework of the social roles, many other topics could be selected.

In developing topics for each role, consideration needs to be given to at least three important perspectives: time dimensions; multiethnic/multicultural comparisons; and local, state, national, and global viewpoints.

From the primary grades on, students should be helped to understand that topics have historical, present, and future dimensions. Although students may not develop an accurate sense of chronology until much later in their schooling, they should leave their elementary years aware and appreciative of the differences and similarities between the past, present, and future.

Students also need to understand and appreciate the multiethnic, multicultural nature of our society and world. This perspective can be encouraged in a social-role organization of elementary social studies by examining topics multiethnically and multiculturally. For example, when considering the worker role at any grade level, likenesses and differences between the work and workers of various ethnic and cultural groups can be examined.

Figure 5

SAMPLE TOPICS FOR K-6 SOCIAL STUDIES

	CITIZEN	WORKER	CONSUMER	FAMILY	FRIENDS	GROUPS	SELF
K-1	Rules Authority School rules laws applicable to children	School Worker Responsibilities Rules Satisfaction	How Advertising Influences Us Television commercials Advertisements in the mall Making choices	What Is A Family? Roles Responsibilities Rules Interdependence of members	Need for Friends Playing with friends Working with friends Feelings about friends	Groups Humans Form Kinds of groups Responsibilities in groups Group rules	What Makes Me Special? Physical characteristics Abilities Feelings
2nd	Citizen Participation: Protecting Our Environment Wise personal use of resources Joining with others in cleanup Choosing wise leaders	Relationship of Geography to Work How natural environment influence work choices Variety of jobs in geographic areas When natural environment causes workers to move	Using Natural Resources: 'Paper' From 'Trees to Paper Conserving our use of paper Recycling paper	Family History Ancestors Traditions Family influence on learning	Conflicts Among Friends Name calling Exclusion Resolving conflicts	Neighborhoods Effect of natural environment on neighborhoods Working together on a neighborhood project Changing neighborhoods	How I Am Like Others Basic needs Basic wants Satisfying needs and wants
3rd	Government Citizen of my city Citizen of my state Citizen of my nation	Need for Work Satisfying personal needs Satisfying needs for goods Satisfying need for progress and problem solutions	Functions of Money Using money to satisfy needs Buying Saving	Use of Family Resources Family members as human resources Conserving energy at home Resolving conflicts about resources	Making New Friends Finding out about a new friend Telling a new friend about yourself Spending time with friends	Ethnic Groups Nature of ethnic groups Immigration and migration Traditions and customs	How I Use My Time Personal interests Personal responsibilities Making choices
4th	Rights Early colonialists commitment to rights Denial of rights Equal Rights Amendment	Tools of Workers Tools in early societies From tools to technology Effect of technology on career choices	Services We Use: Recreation How public recreational services began Private recreational services Using leisure time and services wisely	Changing Roles In Family How family roles have changed over time Working parents Your changing family responsibilities	Being a Friend Helping a friend Loyalty Being yourself while being a friend	Effect of Natural Disasters on Groups Relationship of groups to natural environment Groups' response to crises Interdependence of groups	How My Natural Environment Affects Me Relation to living things How environment affects my activities Affect of natural environment on job choices
5th	Laws How laws are made How laws are enforced How laws are changed	Interdependence of Workers Early workers dependence on others Trade increases interdependence International trade today	Products We Buy: Blue Jeans Levi Strauss "invents" Jeans From cottonfield to store Consumer decisions: buying jeans	Family Likenesses and Differences Likenesses and differences among classmates' families Families around the world	Kinds of Friends Acquaintances Best friends Why friendships change	Clustering of Groups Why people form groups How groups expand How groups change over time	Effects of History on Me Influence of family history Influence of community history Influence of nation's history
6th	Natural Environment and Political Systems Geographic boundaries Political boundaries Interdependence between resources and politics	Workers in History Family Industries Industrialization Worker's rights	Our Future Needs: Oil Sources of oil Other countries viewpoint Present vs future needs	Family Needs: Shelter How natural environment affects shelter decisions How financial resources affect shelter decisions Family moves in	Influence of Friends Learning from friends Behaving like friends Leading and following	Membership in Groups Birth membership Optional membership Effect of groups on members	People I Admire Why we admire others Admiring family and friends Admiring famous people

36

Finally, it is important to help students understand how local, state, national, and global considerations influence people's thoughts and actions. Recent research suggests that global perspectives can be effectively taught even in the primary grades (for example, see Mitsakos 1978). Consideration of a variety of viewpoints is particularly important in studying such current world issues as the oil shortage.

The matrix in Figure 5 shows examples of how all three kinds of perspectives can be included in a K-6 curriculum arranged by social roles. Further examination of the matrix reveals that the topics suggested are, for the most part, not new to social studies programs; indeed, they emerged from our examination of numerous elementary textbook series. Only the role of friend reflects substantially new topics, primarily because that role is seldom considered after the first and second grades in the current curriculum.

Although few of the suggested topics are new, the arrangement of topics is substantially different in the proposed reorganization plan. In the expanding-environment scheme, most of the topics related to the roles of self, family, friend, and, to some extent, group member are currently taught in the primary grades. Topics currently taught in grades 4-6 are related primarily to the citizen role--geographic and historical content which helps students understand and appreciate their nation and world.

In the proposed reorganization around social roles, topics related to all seven social roles would be presented throughout the elementary years. This balanced approach realistically reflects students' perceptions of the world. As a result of watching television, many students-- even in the primary grades--are familiar with world political crises, perhaps more so than with events in their local communities. Their exposure to "the world" in the school curriculum need not wait until the sixth or seventh grade so long as issues are presented in a manner which recognizes students' cognitive, social, and emotional abilities (Torney 1978). Even more importantly, learning about personal social roles-- self, family, and friend--should not cease after grade 3. Social, emotional, and moral development obviously continues after the third grade, but the current curriculum pays only peripheral attention to such development in grades 4-6.

The greatest change brought about by using social roles as an elementary organizer would occur in the fifth-grade social studies program, which is currently a chronological study of U.S. history. In the proposed plan, subject matter would be arranged around social roles. Most students now encounter chronological surveys of U.S. history at three grade levels (5, 8, and 11). All three courses are characterized by much the same content and approach, albeit at different levels of sophistication. In addition to eliminating some repetition of content, organizing grade 5 around social roles would help students understand that people throughout history have played much the same roles, that some of the functions and characteristics of roles have changed over time, and that roles are likely to continue to change in the future. A similar organizational plan could be used for the state history units taught in many fourth-grade classes.

While the theme of seven social roles should be carried through each year, varying amounts of attention can and should be given to different roles in different years. Decisions should be based on both student interest (for example, studying social groups as students start joining Scouts and Little League) and developmental abilities.

Social Roles in Grades 7-12

Social studies in grades 7-12 is generally organized around disciplines of study; history is the most-frequently-taught discipline, followed by geography and political science. In most schools, the other social sciences (psychology, sociology, anthropology, and economics) are taught as electives, if at all. As is the case with the elementary curriculum, the secondary social studies program is held rather firmly in place by text offerings and tradition, in many cases reinforced by state laws, district mandates, and/or professional recommendations.

As with the elementary curriculum, the seven social roles can provide a useful framework for curricular reorganization at the secondary level. However, roles need not be the major organizers for every grade level in the secondary curriculum; instead, a combination of disciplines and social-role organization is suggested. This combination is explained on a grade-by-grade basis below. Examples of topics for grade-level courses are shown in Figure 6.

Figure 6

SAMPLE APPROACHES AND TOPICS FOR 7-12 SOCIAL STUDIES

	SELF	GROUP	FRIENDS	FAMILY	CONSUMER	WORKER	CITIZEN
7th Social Studies (focus on self, family, friends, and group)	Given and earned identities Innate and learned behavior Being alone	Behavioral norms Likenesses and differences among members of a group Likenesses and differences among groups	Friendship and stages of development Same sex friends Opposite sex friends	Relation of family to society Conflict between family and friends Roles in families	Economic wants and needs Personal decisions about use of resources Societal decisions about use of resources	Work opportunities Changes in work opportunities Development of child labor laws	Who decides? (authority) Your rights as a U.S. citizen Your responsibilities as a citizen
8th (U.S. history)	U.S. history organized around seven social roles						
9th Social Studies (focus on worker, consumer, citizen)	Assessing abilities Assessing interests Assessing traits	Kinds of groups socio-economic Influence of groups on identity	Crises in friendship Competition Exclusion	Likenesses and differences among families Differing rules Differing expectations	Supply and Demand Historical changes in supply and demand Future projections for supply and demand	Influence of family on job choices Employer responsibilities Employee responsibilities Social Security	Traffic laws Drug laws Family laws
10th World Cultures	World cultures organized around seven social roles						
11th U.S. History	U.S. history, chronological study						
12th U.S. Government Electives	U.S. Government organized around or with attention to social roles Social Science Elective 1--Interdisciplinary study focusing on self, family, friends, and groups Social Science Elective 2--Interdisciplinary study focusing on consumer, worker, and citizen Social Science Elective 3--Community-based application of social science learning Economics, Psychology, Sociology, Anthropology, Geography--Taught as separate discipline-structured courses						

Seventh Grade

Of all grade levels K-12, the content of social studies in grades 7 and 9 appears to be the least firmly established and perhaps the least satisfactory from both teachers' and students' perspectives (Wiley 1977, p. 30). In grade 7, the typical course offerings may provide a partial explanation. At an age level when students are beginning an intense self-identity search, the typical social studies curriculum offers world history or world geography--subjects far removed from students' immediate concerns. (For a thorough discussion of the early adolescent as learner, see Early Adolescence: Perspectives and Recommendations 1978.) We do not intend to imply that world history and world geography cannot be made meaningful to seventh-graders; however, a review of commonly used textbooks and curriculum guides for grade 7 reveals few connecting links between students' immediate lives and disciplinary studies at that grade level.

As an alternative to the current world history and geography offerings at seventh grade, a continuation of the elementary social-roles organizational scheme is proposed, with topics organized around the seven roles. In this grade, given the immediacy of students' self-awareness needs, topics having relevance for problem analysis and problem solving are suggested. For example, a topic related to the role of self might be "Given and Earned Identities"; for the role of group member, "Behavioral Norms"; for the role of worker, "Development and Current State of Child Labor Laws."

In some respects, this kind of seventh-grade curriculum would repeat the early-elementary-level focus on self-concept and identity. Emerging adolescents in the seventh grade resemble their primary-grade counterparts in that they are entering a new stage of schooling, establishing new roles and relationships in the family, and redefining themselves in relation to the world. Focusing again on these social science topics in seventh grade need not repeat what was taught in the primary grades. Indeed, these topics could be treated in more depth and placed in a more complex social context, thereby representing an application and extension of previous knowledge.

Eighth Grade

Given the prevalence of laws, mandates, and traditions which require the teaching of U.S. history in the eighth grade (or thereabouts) and the importance of history in the development of students' sense of national heritage, it is recommended that a junior-high-level course in U.S. history be taught. However, the importance of teaching a chronological survey of U.S. history at this level is not compelling. The developmental needs of the early adolescent and the fact that most students will have U.S. history again in grade 11 suggest that the eighth-grade course should place less emphasis on chronology and more emphasis on expanding students' understanding of the historical development of the seven social roles.

Several schemes suggest themselves for reorganizing eighth-grade U.S. history. One would be to segment U.S. history into time periods (much as is currently done in survey courses) and to examine within each period how people functioned in their social roles. For example, if the time period were post-World War II, topics might include the national vs. global concerns of postwar citizens, the economic boom which led to the emergence of consumerism, the growth of technology and technology-related careers, the rise of suburbia, changes in family roles, and the changing self-perceptions of men who served abroad in the armed forces and women who left homemaking for paid employment during the war.

The same kind of organizational arrangement could be applied to state and local history courses, which are taught in junior high in some states. Such an arrangement would provide a "social" rather than a "political-military" approach to history, although political and military events would be included. The greatest benefit of such an approach would be to help students compare life across time periods in terms of common social roles.

Ninth Grade

Like the seventh grade, grade 9 seems to lack a clearly defined identity in the social studies curriculum. When many schools moved away from teaching the traditional civics course at this grade level some years ago, no single subject offering emerged to take its place. In some systems, ninth grade became a home for legal, consumer, environmental, or career education. Although the recent proliferation of new civics books on the market may signal the beginning of a return to ninth-grade civics, in 1982 the ninth-grade program is in flux.

To meet the needs of ninth-grade students and to restore focus to this level, we suggest returning to the social roles as the course organizer. At this level, the roles given the most attention would be those of consumer, worker, and citizen. At this age many students are earning money, they are responsible for some consumer decisions, and most have had first-hand experience in working or looking for work. Students are also beginning to come into contact with the legal system through traffic law and, in some cases, unlawful behavior. Thus, learning about societal roles will be personally meaningful to ninth-graders. At this grade level, special attention should be given to such "cross-over" topics as "Family Law" and "Social Security" in order to help students develop an understanding of the interrelatedness and complexity of social roles.

Tenth Grade

In some school systems, social studies is not required of or offered to tenth-graders; in others, students are free to take electives at this grade level. The most common offering is world history. If only one social studies course can be offered in the tenth grade, a world cultures/world history course is suggested--partly in order to comply with the laws and mandates which require such a course but also to ensure that one year in the curriculum will be devoted to development of students' world view. The emphasis should be on world, not Western cultures and on developing as well as developed nations.

A tenth-grade world history course need not be taught strictly as chronological history; it can be organized, to some degree, around social roles. One method of organization would be to explore how roles are filled, historically and currently, in various cultures (a world cultures approach); a second would be to examine how persons in various cultures have played out their roles during different time periods (a chronological approach). As with U.S. history, either of these approaches would result in an approach to world studies that would be primarily social, as opposed to political and military.

Eleventh Grade

Because 81 percent of school districts require students to take U.S. history at about the 11th-grade level (Weiss 1978, p. 24) and because students encounter a great deal of U.S. history content on college entrance examinations, it is suggested that U.S. history be retained at this level, taught in a chronological sequence. As much as possible, it would be useful to draw students' attention to information and insights which are related to their current and future social roles and which will help them understand and appreciate their national heritage.

Twelfth Grade

About one-third of all U.S. school districts require students to take American government in the 12th grade (Weiss 1978, p. 26). The placement of this course in the curriculum—close to students' entry into adult life and political participation—is logical and should be retained. However, social roles can again be used to help focus learning on students' present and future lives. Most U.S. government texts and curriculum guides are organized according to governmental structures or processes. If those organizers are retained, social roles can be used within the study of a typical topic—for example, bureaucracy—to show how bureaucratic processes are related to being a consumer, citizen, worker, family member, and so on. A more radical approach would be to organize the course around social roles—relating applicable political science and civics content to each of the seven roles.

Senior High Electives

In senior high schools large enough to support social science electives, the most-commonly-offered courses are economics, psychology, sociology, and some variation of problems of democracy (Weiss 1978). Most economics, sociology, and psychology courses follow a structure-of-the-discipline approach that is more academic than applied. Although such courses provide a useful introduction for students who are preparing to take college courses in the disciplines, they may be less meaningful to students who will do no further study in these discipline areas.

If a school is able to offer only one or two elective social studies/social science offerings, these courses should combine knowledge and skills from two or more social sciences and should be organized around social roles. One such course might focus on personal roles: self, family, friend, group member. A fruitful topic for consideration might be "Life Cycles"--personal, family, friend, and career. Concepts and skills taught would draw heavily from psychology, sociology, anthropology, and, to a lesser extent, political science and economics. Other possible topics might be "Learning" as it applies to academic, career, and leisure settings and "Interpersonal Relationships" as experienced in the family, among friends, and on the job.

A second interdisciplinary social studies elective might focus on the roles of worker, consumer, and citizen. Subject matter for this course would be heavily drawn from economics, geography, and political science, with lesser amounts from sociology, psychology, and anthropology. Possible topics would include "Economic Cycles" as related to consumers and workers, "Interdependence of Employment and Consumption," and "Citizen Rights and Responsibilities."

A third elective might focus on social roles in the community, broadening students' understanding of how people function in their roles and how various roles are interrelated. Course content would be learned through community participation--perhaps via student internships in government, business, or social-service agencies. Knowledge and skills from all the social sciences could be used to help students analyze and more effectively participate in out-of-school experiences.

Such interdisciplinary electives are proposed instead of traditional, discipline-oriented studies when only a limited number of social studies/social science electives can be offered. If possible, it would also be desirable for a school to offer one or more discipline-based courses in sociology, psychology, economics, geography, or anthropology for students who wish to study the structures of particular disciplines and the methodology of social scientists.

Looking at the Proposed K-12 Curriculum

By combining the elementary and secondary matrices in Figures 5 and 6, a complete K-12 curriculum organization scheme can be seen. Even a quick perusal reveals that the scheme combines elements of the currently prevailing social studies pattern with some innovations.

At the K-3 level, the suggested changes do not represent new content so much as rearrangement and changes in emphasis. The greatest changes are suggested for grades 4-6, the junior-high level, and senior-high electives, because dissatisfaction in the field seems most pronounced at these grade levels. Although content has been specified by grade level, specific course placement could be rearranged to accommodate local requirements or tradition.

The following advantages would ensue from this suggested organizational scheme:

First, emphasis on social roles at all grade levels would add continuity and a unifying dimension to the social studies curriculum that is not present in the current pattern. The schism between the interdisciplinary elementary program and the discipline-centered secondary organization would be resolved. The practice of presenting U.S. history survey courses at three different grade levels would be abandoned in favor of providing more historical perspectives in each elementary grade, emphasizing historical roles in grade 8, and offering a chronological study in the 11th grade.

Second, we believe that because the proposed scheme is more responsive to the ways in which information is acquired by students in their everyday lives, it would better prepare them to use knowledge and skills from social studies to effectively participate in their social world. We have no empirical evidence to support this theory because such an orientation has never been tried; however, we hope that our proposal will stimulate the research and curriculum development needed to test such a scheme.

Finally, the proposed scheme provides a structure for organizing social studies that will be useful but not limiting. This scheme provides course frameworks but does not dictate or delimit topics or skills. Although examples are suggested, many other topics could be substituted.

This discussion of social studies organized around seven social roles has assumed a pure application of the scheme. However, at this point a pure application is not a realistic possibility because no curriculum materials which organize social studies content in this manner exist. We hope that materials developers, along with school districts, will consider this proposal and begin to develop products incorporating some of these ideas.

Meanwhile, a social-role orientation could be useful to school systems that are presently evaluating, developing, or redesigning their social studies programs. If, for example, a district is evaluating its current program, social roles could provide a lens through which to view the program, suggesting such questions as these: How much does the K-12 curriculum contribute to students' understanding of and more effective participation (current and future) in the seven social roles? Where do deficiencies exist? How can they be remedied? If teaching about a particular role seems deficient at a particular grade, a unit of study on that role could be developed by pulling together a variety of resources--supplementary materials, parts of texts, multimedia--and infusing the resulting unit into the existing program. If there is substantial dissatisfaction with the social studies program at a particular grade level, a different course could be designed around roles by adapting available resources or writing new materials.

Is a curriculum reorganization effort worthwhile? Obviously, the task would be difficult. Any curriculum reform involving substantial change must consider laws, accreditation, competency exams, and teacher training in addition to the necessity of preparing local and state guides, developing and distributing curriculum materials, and, most important, selling the idea to educators and the public (who have had 60 years to get accustomed to the present curriculum). There are also the questions of whether the current organizational plan warrants a change and whether evidence suggests that an alternative plan would be better.

Although the answers to these questions are not clear-cut, the widespread dissatisfaction with social studies expressed by students and teachers suggests a need to look at each aspect of social studies education. We believe that the current curriculum pattern warrants reconsideration. By suggesting that social roles represent a potentially powerful organizer for social studies, we hope to challenge the field of social studies to reconsider the prevailing K-12 curriculum pattern, think about the proposed framework for reorganization, consider the grade-by-grade course content suggestions, and actively debate and hopefully agree on an organizational scheme that will better meet current and future needs in social studies education.

SOCIAL ROLES: THE MAIN IDEAS

Citizen

A citizen is a person who owes allegiance to, is entitled to certain rights from, and has certain responsibilities to a sovereign power or political entity.

Every person is a citizen of several political communities, including the neighborhood, city, state, and nation. One's relationship to the entire world can also be viewed as that of a global citizen.

Citizens in the United States engage in several mandatory activities, including paying taxes, obeying laws, and (in times of draft) serving in the armed forces.

Citizens in the United States also engage in various voluntary activities, including voting, advocating positions, working for political organizations, working for political candidates, finding out about public issues, and holding public office.

At times our roles as citizens of the various political communities conflict. (Example: having to decide whether to support the development of coal mines in Colorado to increase the energy reserves of the nation or to oppose such action in order to protect the ecology and environment of the state.)

Being a responsible, competent citizen in the United States also involves being able to perform important thinking skills, such as acquiring and interpreting information about political institutions and public issues and making thoughtful decisions about public policy issues.

Being a responsible, competent citizen in the United States involves being able to perform certain vital participatory skills, such as communicating one's ideas and views clearly and working effectively as an individual and in groups to act on those views.

Being a responsible, competent citizen in the United States involves understanding and making commitments to the basic democratic values embodied in our Constitution and resolving conflicts among these values in rational, humane ways.

The role of citizen is closely related to other social roles. (Example: as consumers, we may also work with organized groups to influence government policy.)

At times the role of citizen conflicts with other social roles. (Example: a political official who gives special favors to a friend at the public's expense has experienced a conflict between his or her role as a public official and as a personal friend.)

Worker

A worker is one who engages in a conscious effort--usually for pay--to produce goods, services, and ideas for the benefit of oneself and/or others.

Most persons in our society are workers, but their work roles change over the life cycle. (Example: adolescents may hold part-time jobs; most adults have full-time jobs and change jobs several times during their working lives; many older persons earn benefits as retired workers.)

The activities of workers have changed throughout history and will continue to change as technology, availability of resources, human wants and needs, and other factors change. (Example: primitive persons were primarily hunters and gatherers; the Industrial Revolution generated the need for assembly-line workers; sophisticated technology has produced specialists among workers.)

To do his or her work, a worker depends on financial and material resources, the labor of other workers, and consumer demand. (Example: the work of a General Motors factory worker depends on such factors as the company's ability to get necessary materials and equipment, the labor of other workers who convert natural resources into usable materials, and the American public's interest in buying General Motors automobiles.)

Although workers in our society are free to choose the work they do, certain laws regulate work rights and responsibilities for both employers and employees. (Example: minimum wage laws require most workers to be paid at least $3.35 per hour.)

The worker role affects and is affected by the other six roles. (Example: work colleagues often become off-the-job friends.)

A person's worker role can conflict with one or more of his or her other social roles. (Example: a worker may find his or her assigned work schedule in conflict with a holiday of the religious group to which he or she belongs.)

Productive work can be a source of satisfaction as well as income.

Wise decisions about career choices require knowledge about jobs and clarification of personal values.

Competent workers demonstrate effective skills, job knowledge, decision-making ability, and appropriate attitudes and work habits.

Consumer

All persons are consumers.

The function of the consumer is to buy and/or use the resources, goods, and services produced in nature and in the marketplace.

Consumers buy and/or use natural resources (water, wood, oil, gas); manufactured products (food, drugs, bicycles, cars); information (print and other media); business services (banking, insurance, real estate); and social services (education, medicine, recreation, welfare).

Consumer behavior influences production of goods and services, and production influences consumer behavior (the law of supply and demand).

Consumer wants and needs have changed throughout history and will continue to change in the future because of changes in technology, availability of natural resources, financial conditions, lifestyles, and other factors.

What we consume and how we consume affects us as individuals, others in our society, and ultimately all persons on earth.

Although consumer wants and needs vary from society to society, all consumers on earth are interdependent because our global resources are finite.

The consumer role affects and is affected by each of the other six roles, and this interrelationship sometimes leads to conflict. (Example: a father's personal want to buy a sports car may conflict with his fatherly want to send his daughter to an expensive college.)

An individual's wants and needs change throughout the life cycle. (Example: a child's want for candy changes to a want for hamburgers in adolescence and for prime rib in adulthood.)

A competent consumer is a good planner, good shopper, protector of goods and services, and an effective money manager.

Family Member

A family in the strict sociological sense is a group of people related by birth, marriage, or adoption who live together for the primary purposes of procreation and child rearing.

The term family is also used in a broader sense to include extended relationships (e.g., aunts and uncles) and alternative styles (e.g., married couple living together without children).

While many people think of the typical American family as two adults and two children, American families actually come in a wide variety of sizes and forms. (Examples: single parent, single child, no child, many children.)

The role of family member consists of several specific and inter-related sub-roles--mother, father, husband, wife, son, daughter, brother, and sister--each carrying particular rights and responsibilities.

Families satisfy a number of basic needs, including love, caring, food, shelter, and clothing.

The nature of relationships within families varies from culture to culture and from period to period throughout history. (Example: the degree of authoritarianism that a parent exhibits toward a child has varied throughout history and is different in various cultures.)

A person's role in the family changes as he or she grows from infant to child, adolescent, and adult.

Family members are sometimes involved in conflicts related to their different roles within the family.

The nature and composition of one's family may change over time due to death and divorce.

The role of family member is closely related to other social roles. (Example: much of one's role as consumer occurs within the context of the family; membership in ethnic and religious groups has a major impact on the nature of one's family.)

At times one's role as a family member conflicts with other social roles. (Examples: the single mother who would like to stay home to care for her sick child but who also needs to be at an important meeting at work; a husband who spends considerable time with male friends at the expense of his relationship with his wife.)

Friend

Friends are companions bound by affection and esteem, who share experiences, thoughts, and feelings with one another.

There are many different kinds and levels of friendships, ranging from casual to intimate. These include convenience friends (e.g., co-worker), "doing things" friends (e.g., going to movies together), milestone friends (e.g., former college roommates), mentor friends (e.g., those you can go to for advice), and close friends (mutual and open sharing with one another).

Certain factors help build and maintain friendships. These include trusting, being open, sharing experiences, providing help when needed, allowing individuality, accepting one another, showing loyalty, keeping confidences, displaying warmth and affection, being honest, and having fun together.

The nature and bases of friendship change over time and throughout the life cycle. (Example: children's friendships appear to evolve through the following stages: momentary playmates, one-way assistance, two-way cooperation, mutual sharing, and autonomy and interdependence.)

Friendship satisfies a wide variety of important personal and societal needs, including affection, warmth, acceptance, belongingness, happiness, and (according to some recent evidence) good health.

Being a friend involves maintaining some rights (e.g., to retain some privacy and independence) and fulfilling some responsibilities (e.g., being there when your friend needs you).

Conflicts can occur even among good friends. Good friends can deal with these conflicts openly without destroying their relationships. Sometimes resolving conflicts can lead to even closer friendships.

Friendships can develop between members of the opposite sexes (some that involve sexual activity and some that do not) and among people of different ethnic groups and cultures. Some friendships also develop between persons of different ages.

Friendships often grow out of other roles and are reinforced by those relationships. (Example: children usually develop their friendships from relationships with classmates in school or fellow members of a band or athletic team; co-workers often become friends; members of one's family can also be good friends.)

At times the role of friend can conflict with other roles. (Example: co-workers who are also friends may find it difficult to criticize each other's work, even though that would be the best practice for their jobs.)

Member of Social Groups

All persons are members of social groups, either by birth or by choice.

At birth, all persons become members of the male or female sex, a racial group, and an age cohort group.

Persons are born into groups such as religious groups, ethnic groups, and socioeconomic classes, but they may later choose to reject involvement in these groups or may change to other groups.

Persons choose to belong to social or civic groups. (Examples: bridge clubs, baseball teams, and women's consciousness-raising groups.)

All persons are members of social aggregates which are groups without formal organization. (Examples: males in the United States, students in the world, mountain dwellers, suburban dwellers.)

The size and functions of social groups vary; some groups are small, face-to-face groups (e.g., bridge clubs), while some groups have thousands of members (e.g., Jews, National Association for the Advancement of Colored People); some groups are purely social (e.g., a gourmet dinner club), while others have particular goals for the maintenance or improvement of the group (e.g., National Organization of Women).

Persons choose to participate in social groups as much or as little as they wish. (Example: some members of the Catholic religion attend mass each day; other Catholics seldom go to mass.)

Social groups have certain socially prescribed expectations and norms for their members. (Example: members of athletic teams are expected to attend practice sessions.)

Social groups are affected by and affect the course of historical events. (Examples: the impact of the Civil War on blacks; the role of the Women's Christian Temperance Union in passing the Eighteenth Amendment.)

Social groups are affected by and affect each other, sometimes in cooperation and sometimes in conflict. (Examples: ethnic groups joining together to provide language instruction for new immigrants; Jewish Defense League in conflict with the Ku Klux Klan.)

Because social groups have differing expectations for members, an individual who belongs to more than one social group may find expectations of those groups in conflict. (Example: a woman belonging to an orthodox religion may find her religion's teachings in conflict with NOW's philosophy.)

The role of social group member affects and is affected by the other six social roles. (Example: a woman's ethnic background affects the way in which she parents her children.)

Social groups make contributions to both individual members and to society. (Example: a Boy Scout gains self-esteem by participating in his den's camp-out; the Boy Scouts beautify their city's parks by picking up litter.)

Self

The primary role of self is the development of one's full potentialities as a unique and competent person.

On the one hand, our society with its focus on the individual encourages the full development of one's self; on the other hand, it also requires that the person conform to societal expectations related to each of the roles.

An important aspect of the role of self is becoming more aware of one's own likes and dislikes, interests, needs, and values.

Another vital aspect of the role of self is developing a positive and realistic self-concept--knowing who you are and feeling good about yourself. Successful functioning helps build self-esteem.

Another key aspect of this role is expanding one's intellectual capacities to the fullest.

Another important aspect is developing and maintaining physical and emotional well-being.

One's self develops through a series of stages as one moves through the life cycle. These stages generally progress from egocentric to conformist to autonomous to integrative orientations.

The role of self is closely related to the other social roles. Part of a person's identity, perhaps most of it, is defined and derived from his or her roles as female (or male), worker, consumer, parent (or child), friend, citizen, and member of an ethnic group. Much of the striving for self-fulfillment occurs within these roles (e.g., becoming the best teacher possible).

The role of self also involves engaging in activities beyond the other social roles for pure personal satisfaction, enjoyment, and enhancement. (Examples: leisurely reading a book, swimming or running to feel fit, or backpacking by oneself in the mountains.)

At times our personal and individual needs and desires conflict with those related to the other social roles. (Example: a man's desire and need to run five miles a day after work for his personal betterment may conflict with his need as a husband and father to help prepare dinner.)

SOCIAL ROLES: RELATING THE MAIN IDEAS TO TOPICS AND COURSES

Citizen

1. A citizen is a person who owes allegiance to, is entitled to certain rights from, and has certain responsibilities to a sovereign power or political entity.

U.S. History	The Revolutionary War and the new nation-- from subject to citizen
Government	Citizen rights and responsibilities in the U.S. Constitution
World Cultures	Citizenship in different countries

2. Every person is a citizen of several political communities, including the neighborhood, city, state, and nation. One's relationship to the entire world can also be viewed as that of a global citizen.

U.S. History	States' rights vs. federal government issues in the 1840s-1860s
Government	Local, state, and federal governments and the interrelationships among them
Contemporary Issues	Global issues that transcend national boundaries (e.g., energy, population, and inflation)

3. Citizens in the United States engage in several mandatory activities, including paying taxes, obeying laws, and (in times of draft) serving in the armed forces.

U.S. History	Taxation without representation (American Revolution), civil disobedience, the draft in U.S. wars
Government	The courts and justice system
Law-related Education	Citizen rights and responsibilities under the law
Economics	Taxation

4. Citizens in the United States also engage in various voluntary activities including voting, advocating positions, working for political organizations, working for political candidates, finding out about public issues, and holding public office.

U.S. History	Women's suffrage, civil rights, peace movements, political parties throughout U.S. history, Peace Corps
Government	Voting behavior, political parties, pressure groups, elected officials
World Cultures	Political participation in different countries

5. At times our roles as citizens of the various political communities conflict.

U.S. History	League of Nations controversy, secession and civil war
Government	Federal vs. state and local authority in civil rights
Contemporary Issues	Resource development in Rocky Mountains (environment of west vs. national energy needs)

6. Being a responsible, competent citizen in the United States also involves being able to perform important thinking skills, such as acquiring and interpreting information about political institutions and public issues and making thoughtful decisions about public policy issues.

Government	Referendum issues (e.g., school taxes, mass transit)
Contemporary Issues	All political and social issues

7. Being a responsible, competent citizen in the United States involves being able to perform certain vital participatory skills, such as communicating one's ideas and views clearly and working effectively as an individual and in groups to act on those views.

Government	Mock trials, debates, and community work

8. Being a responsible, competent citizen in the United States involves understanding and making commitments to the basic democratic values embodied in our Constitution and resolving conflicts among these values in rational, humane ways.

U.S. History	New Deal--social welfare vs. free enterprise
Government	Supreme Court cases (e.g., Marbury vs. Madison, Dred Scott, Brown vs. Board of Education)

9. The role of citizen is closely related to other social roles.

    U.S. History   Anti-trust laws in late 19th century

    Government   Government regulation of employment (e.g.,
                          child labor laws), consumer rights groups,
                          ERA impact on families, protection of minority
                          groups' rights by the government

10. At times the role of citizen conflicts with other social roles.

    U.S. History   Teapot Dome scandal (citizen vs. friend),
                          duty to go to war vs. duty to family in World
                          Wars I and II

Worker

1. A worker is one who engages in a conscious effort--usually for pay--
    to produce goods, services, and ideas for the benefit of oneself
    and/or others.

    Economics   Goods and services, human resources, market,
                          free enterprise vs. mixed economy, entre-
                          preneurship, management, wages

2. Most persons in our society are workers, but their work roles change
    over the life cycle.

    Psychology   Attitudes toward work

    Economics   Adolescents in the work force, changes in
                          jobs over the life cycle

    Government   Social Security

3. The activities of workers have changed throughout history and will
    continue to change as technology, availability of resources, human
    wants and needs, and other factors change.

    History/Economics   Primitive persons were primarily hunters and
                          gatherers, cottage industries held families
                          together, the Industrial Revolution generated
                          the need for assembly-line workers, sophis-
                          ticated technology has produced specialists

57

U.S. History   The Depression and WPA

4. To do his or her work, a worker depends on financial and material
    resources, the labor of other workers, and consumer demand.

    Economics   Productive resources: human, natural, and
                           capital; supply of and demand for, goods and
                           labor; unemployment

    U.S. History   The Depression, post-World War II industrial
                           boom

5. Although workers in our society are free to choose the work they
    do, certain laws regulate work rights and responsibilities for both
    employers and employees.

    Government   Minimum wage laws, regulatory agencies

    U.S. History   Right-to-work legislation, sweat shops, child
                           labor laws

    Economics   Wage and price controls

6. The worker role affects and is affected by the other six roles.

    History   The early agricultural period and the cottage
                           industry period made families financially
                           interdependent; feudal period in European
                           history linked work and family roles

    Sociology   Work colleagues often became off-the-job
                           friends, social groups and work stereotypes
                           (Irish as policemen, Jewish merchants)

    Psychology   Career and self-identity

7. A person's worker role can conflict with one or more of his or her
    other social roles.

    Government   Legislative debate on government funding of
                           day-care center for working parents, union
                           expectation that members will vote for cer-
                           tain political candidates

    History   Evolution of the eight-hour work day as a
                           response to worker demand for more personal
                           and family time

| Psychology | Worker burnout, conflicts between job and self-concept |

8. Productive work can be a source of satisfaction as well as income.

Psychology	Workaholics
Sociology	Volunteerism
World Cultures	Totalitarian vs. democratic views of work satisfaction

9. Wise decisions about career choices require knowledge about jobs and clarification of personal values.

| Career Education | Taking inventory of personal abilities and interests |
| Economics | Consumer decisions |

10. Competent workers demonstrate effective skills, job knowledge, decision-making ability, and appropriate attitudes and work habits.

| Career Education | Decision-making process and career development |
| Psychology | The psychology of work and job satisfaction |

Consumer

1. All persons are consumers.

| Economics | Theory of consumption and the industrial system |

2. The function of the consumer is to buy and/or use the resources, goods, and services produced in nature and in the marketplace.

| Economics | Theory of consumption, distribution of goods and services |
| Geography | Resources in the United States and world |

3. Consumers buy and/or use natural resources (water, wood, oil, gas); manufactured products (food, drugs, bicycles, cars); information (print and other media); business services (banking, insurance, real estate); and social services (education, medicine, recreation, welfare).

   Consumer Economics   Types of consumer goods

   Contemporary Issues   Global resources, private vs. public responsibility for social services

4. Consumer behavior influences production of goods and services, and production influences consumer behavior.

   Economics   Theory of supply and demand, consumer equilibrium, inflation

   Sociology/   Consumer behavior, influences on consumer
     Psychology   demand

5. Consumer wants and needs have changed throughout history and will continue to change in the future because of changes in technology, availability of natural resources, financial conditions, lifestyles, and other factors.

   Economics   Exchange of goods and services

   U.S. History   Rationing during world wars, mass production

   Government   Sumptuary laws, taxes on and subsidies for consumer goods

6. What we consume and how we consume affects us as individuals, others in our society, and ultimately all persons on earth.

   Economics/   Balance of payments in trade, fishing rights
     U.S. History

   Contemporary Issues   Energy, global interdependence, water rights, conflicts among states

7. Although consumer wants and needs vary from society to society, all consumers on earth are interdependent because our global resources are finite.

   Contemporary Issues   Ecology and the environment, energy and natural resources

   Economics   Inflation and depression

8. The consumer role affects and is affected by each of the other six roles, and this interrelationship sometimes leads to conflict.

   U.S./World History   Class conflicts based on different abilities to consume (due to income inequality)

9. An individual's wants and needs change throughout the life cycle.

   U.S. History/   School lunches, Social Security, Medicare
   Government

10. A competent consumer is a good planner, good shopper, protector of goods and services, and an effective money manager.

   Consumer Economics   Consumer abilities and functions

Family Member

1. A family in the strict sociological sense is a group of people related by birth, marriage, or adoption who live together for the primary purposes of procreation and child rearing.

   Sociology   Family functions, family traditions and customs

2. The term family is also used in a broader sense to include extended relationships (e.g., aunts and uncles) and alternative styles (e.g., married couple living together without children).

   Sociology   Extended families, effect of mobility on extended families

   U.S. History   Impact of World War II on extended families

3. While many people think of the typical American family as two adults and two children, American families actually come in a wide variety of sizes and forms.

   Sociology   Single parenting, marriage and cohabitation

   Government   Child abuse laws, alimony in cohabitation

4. The role of family member consists of several specific and inter-related sub-roles--mother, father, husband, wife, son, daughter, brother, and sister--each carrying particular rights and responsibilities.

    Sociology   Family roles, family size, position of siblings

    Government   Legal responsibilities (e.g., child support)

5. Families satisfy a number of basic needs, including love, caring, food, shelter, and clothing.

    Economics   Responsibility for providing basic needs

    Government   Government assistance to families

    U.S. History   History of child advocacy legislation

6. The nature of relationships within families varies from culture to culture and from period to period throughout history.

    World Cultures   Tradition of marriage in various cultures, authoritarianism in child rearing across cultures

    U.S. History   Changing family composition, lifestyles, responsibilities, and expectations

7. A person's role in the family changes as he or she grows from infant to child, adolescent, and adult.

    Psychology   Self-identity in changing family roles

8. Family members are sometimes involved in conflicts related to their different roles within the family.

    Economics   Consumer decisions related to family needs

    Government   Family law

    Sociology/Psychology   Dual-career marriages

9. The nature and composition of one's family may change over time due to death and divorce.

    Government   Divorce laws, inheritance laws

Sociology/Psychology Nursing home care

    U.S. History   How families have dealt with aging members in
                          various periods of history

    World Cultures   How various cultures have dealt with aging
                          family members

10. The role of family member is closely related to other social roles.

    Economics   Family consumer decision making

    Sociology   Ethnic background's effect on marriage (e.g.,
                        arranged marriages)

11. At times one's role as a family member conflicts with other social
     roles.

    Career Education   Careers and working mothers

    Government   Tax structure which favors single persons
                        over married persons

Friend

Since each of the main ideas about friends can be taught in relation to the following topics and courses, we have listed them only once.

1. Friends are companions bound by affection and esteem, who share
    experiences, thoughts, and feelings with one another.

2. There are many different kinds and levels of friendships ranging
    from casual to intimate. These include convenience friends (e.g.,
    co-worker), "doing things" friends (e.g., going to movies together),
    milestone friends (e.g., former college roommates), mentor friends
    (e.g., those you can go to for advice), and close friends (mutual
    and open sharing with one another).

3. Certain factors help build and maintain friendships. These include
    trusting, being open, sharing experiences, providing help when
    needed, allowing individuality, accepting one another, showing
    loyalty, keeping confidences, displaying warmth and affection, being
    honest, and having fun together.

4. The nature and bases of friendships change over time and throughout
    the life cycle.

5. Friendship satisfies a wide variety of important personal and soci-
    etal needs, including affection, warmth, acceptance, belongingness,
    happiness, and (according to some recent evidence) good health.

6. Being a friend involves maintaining some rights (e.g., to retain
    some privacy and independence) and fulfilling some responsibilities
    (e.g., being there when your friend needs you).

7. Conflicts can occur even among good friends. Good friends can deal
    with these conflicts openly without destroying their relationships.
    Sometimes resolving conflicts can lead to even closer friendship.

8. Friendships can develop between males and females (some that involve
    sexual activity and some that do not) and among people of different
    ethnic groups and cultures. Some friendships also develop between
    persons of different ages.

9. Friendships often grow out of other roles and are reinforced by
    those relationships.

10. At times the role of friend can conflict with other roles.

For all main ideas 1-10:

Psychology	Affection and esteem Stages of friendship
Sociology	Interpersonal relationships Effects of social mobility on friendships
U.S. History	Friendship relationships and issues involving friends in conflict (e.g., McCarthy hearings, friends in movie business testifying against one another; Presidents, like Harding, who appointed his friends to many cabinet positions; friendships that grew out of wartime experiences)
Government	The press and politicians (can they be friends?)

Member of Social Groups

1. All persons are members of social groups, either by birth or by
    choice.

Sociology	Primary and secondary groups, norms, groups, culture

2. At birth, all persons become members of the male or female sex, a racial group, and an age cohort group.

    Psychology   Feminine and masculine roles

    Sociology   Peer groups, aging, race and ethnicity

    Government   Social legislation, such as that protecting the elderly and dependent children; anti-discrimination legislation

3. Persons are born into groups such as religious groups, ethnic groups, and socioeconomic classes, but they may later choose to reject involvement in these groups or may change to other groups.

    Sociology   Class and caste, social mobility

    U.S. History   Pluralism and assimilation

4. Persons choose to belong to social or civic groups.

    Psychology   Group membership and self-identity

    Sociology   American social system, channels of social mobility, bases of stratification

5. All persons are members of social aggregates which are groups without formal organization.

    Geography   Population distribution, effect of climate and terrain on dwellers

    Sociology   Urban vs. rural dwellers

6. The size and functions of social groups vary; some groups are small, face-to-face groups (e.g., bridge clubs), while some groups have thousands of members (e.g., Jews, National Association for the Advancement of Colored People); some groups are purely social (e.g., gourmet dinner clubs), while others have particular goals for the maintenance or improvement of the group (e.g., National Organization of Women).

    Psychology   Self-identity and social group membership

    Sociology   Socialization, power, influence

7. Persons choose to participate in social groups as much or as little
    as they wish.

    Sociology   Group dynamics, group influence on behavior

    Anthropology   Cultural traits

    Psychology   Conformity and free choice

8. Social groups have certain socially-prescribed expectations and
    norms for their members.

    Sociology   Group dynamics, creeds, membership rituals

    Anthropology   Acculturation, values and belief systems of
                             various cultural groups

9. Social groups are affected by and affect the course of historical
    events.

    U.S. History   Pilgrims and religious persecution, effect of
                             Civil War on blacks, American Indians and
                             Westward expansion, Japanese internment camps,
                             Vietnamese immigration

10. Social groups are affected by and affect each other, sometimes in
    cooperation and sometimes in conflict.

    U.S. History   Salem witch trials

    Government   Volunteerism, ethnic groups joining together
                             to provide language instruction for new immi-
                             grants

    Sociology   Racism, clashes between the Jewish Defense
                             League and the Ku Klux Klan

11. Because social groups have differing expectations for members, an
    individual who belongs to more than one social group may find expec-
    tations of those groups in conflict.

    Psychology   Role conflict

12. The role of social group member affects and is affected by the other
    six social roles.

    Career Education   Job choices are affected by membership in age
                             group, sex group, heritage group, and socio-
                             economic status

Sociology	Parenting, how ethnic background affects the way one parents a child
History	Immigration, clustering of new immigrants in housing and jobs
Government	Voting patterns, affected by ethnic group clusters and by geographic aggregation (e.g., urban vs. rural voters)

13. Social groups make contributions to both individual members and to society.

Sociology/Psychology	Delinquency, how group membership can lead to or reinforce negative behavior
U.S. History	Ethnic history and contributions to the building of America

Self

1. The primary role of self is the development of one's full potentialities as a unique and competent person.

Psychology	Personality, self, self-actualization

2. On the one hand, our society with its focus on the individual encourages the full development of one's self; on the other hand, it also requires that the person conform to societal expectations related to each of the roles.

Sociology	Roles and statuses in the social structure, socialization, class and stratification, conformity vs. individuality
Psychology	Individualization, the individual in society

3. An important aspect of the role of self is becoming more aware of one's own likes and dislikes, interests, needs, and values.

Psychology	Needs, motivation, interests, attitudes, and values

4. Another vital aspect of the role of self is developing a positive and realistic self-concept--knowing who you are and feeling good about yourself. Successful functioning helps build self-esteem.

Sociology	Prestige and esteem related to roles
Psychology	Self-concept

67

5. Another key aspect of this role is expanding one's intellectual capacities to the fullest.

    Psychology   Emotions, intelligence, physiological foundations of behavior

    Other social studies   Learning in U.S. history, world history,
      courses   economics, and other social studies courses to expand one's knowledge about the social world

6. Another important aspect is developing and maintaining physical and emotional well-being.

    Psychology   Emotions, intelligence, physiological foundations of behavior

    Other social studies   Learning in U.S. history, world history,
      courses   economics, and other social studies courses to expand one's knowledge about the social world

7. One's self develops through a series of stages as one moves through the life cycle. These stages generally progress from egocentric to conformist to autonomous to integrative orientations.

    Psychology   Child development, adolescent development, adult development, ego development, moral and intellectual development.

8. The role of self is closely related to the other social roles. Part of a person's identity, perhaps most of it, is defined and derived from his or her roles as female (or male) worker, consumer, parent (or child), friend, citizen, and member of an ethnic group. Much of the striving for self-fulfillment occurs within these roles (e.g., becoming the best teacher possible).

    Sociology   Work organization, male and female roles, caste and class, the family, government and political sociology, racial and ethnic identity

    Social Psychology   How groups influence behavior, the effect of interpersonal relationships on self-concept

9. The role of self also involves engaging in activities beyond the other social roles for pure personal satisfaction, enjoyment, and enhancement.

    Sociology   Societal expectations vs. personal needs

    Psychology   Self-actualization vs. socialization

10. At times our personal and individual needs and desires conflict with those related to the other social roles.

    Sociology   Societal expectations vs. personal needs

    Psychology   Self-actualization vs. socialization

REFERENCES

Anderson, Lee (1982). "Barriers to Change in Social Studies." In The Current State of Social Studies: A Report of Project Span. Boulder, Colo.: Social Science Education Consortium.

Barr, Robert D., James L. Barth, and S. Samuel Shermis (1977). Defining the Social Studies. Arlington, Va.: National Council for the Social Studies.

Berelson, Bernard (1962). "Introduction." In The Social Studies and the Social Sciences. New York: Harcourt, Brace, and World.

Bigge, Morris L. (1971). Positive Relativism: An Emergent Educational Philosophy. New York: Harper and Row.

Block, Joel D. (1980). Friendship. New York: Macmillan.

Blumer, Herbert (1970). "Sociological Implications of the Thought of George Herbert Mead." In Gregory P. Stone and Harvey A. Farberman, eds., Social Psychology Through Symbolic Interactionism. Waltham, Mass.: Ginn-Blaisdell.

Butts, R. Freeman (1979). "The Revival of Civic Learning: A Rationale for the Education of Citizens." Social Education 43, no. 5 (May 1979), pp. 359-364.

Canfield, Jack, and Harold G. Wells (1976). 100 Ways to Enhance Self-Concept. Englewood Cliffs, N.J.: Prentice-Hall.

Cole, Sheila (1980). "Send Our Children to Work?" Psychology Today 14, no. 2 (July 1980), pp. 44-68.

Dufty, David (1980). "Living Skills as a Core Curriculum Component." Sydney: University of Sydney.

Early Adolescence: Perspectives and Recommendations (1978). Washington, D.C.: National Science Foundation.

Farman, Greg, Gary Natriello, and Sanford M. Dornbusch (1978). "Social Studies and Motivation: High School Students' Perceptions of the Articulation of Social Studies to Work, Family, and Community." Theory and Research in Social Education 6, no. 3 (September 1978), pp. 27-39.

Fenton, Edwin (1977). "The Implications of Lawrence Kohlberg's Research for Civic Education." In B. Frank Brown, director, Education for Responsible Citizenship. New York: McGraw-Hill.

Fontana, Lynn (1980). Perspectives on the Social Studies. Research Report no. 78. Bloomington, Ind.: Agency for Instructional Television.

71

Foshay, Arthur W., and William W. Burton (1976). "Citizenship as the Aim of Social Studies." Theory and Research in Social Education 4, no. 2 (December 1976), pp. 1-22.

Gallup, George H. (1978). "The Tenth Annual Gallup Poll of the Public's Attitudes Toward the Public Schools." Phi Delta Kappan 60, no. 1 (September), pp. 33-45.

Gallup, George H. (1979). "The Eleventh Annual Gallup Poll of the Public's Attitudes Toward the Public Schools." Phi Delta Kappan 61, no. 1 (September), pp. 33-46.

Haas, John D. (1980). "Society, Social Justice, and Social/Political Education: A Reaction." In Irving Morrissett and Ann M. Williams, eds., Social/Political Education in Three Countries. Boulder, Colo.: ERIC Clearinghouse for Social Studies/Social Science Education and Social Science Education Consortium, Inc.

Hertzberg, Hazel W. (1981). Social Studies Reform: 1880-1980. Report of Project SPAN. Boulder, Colo.: Social Science Education Consortium.

Joyce, William W., and Janet E. Alleman-Brooks (1979). Teaching Social Studies in the Elementary and Middle Schools. New York: Holt, Rinehart and Winston.

Kitchens, James A., and Raymond H. Muessig (1980). The Study and Teaching of Sociology. Columbus, Ohio: Charles E. Merrill.

Marker, Gerald W. (1980). "Goals for Political and Social Participation." Journal of Research and Development in Education 31, no. 2 (Winter), pp. 72-81.

Martin, John Henry (1980). "Reconsidering the Goals of High School Education." Educational Leadership 37, no. 4 (January 1980), pp. 278-285.

Martorella, Peter H. (1979). "Part II, Research in Social Studies Education: Implications for Teaching in the Cognitive Domain." Social Education 43, no. 7 (November/December), pp. 599-601.

Mendlovitz, Saul H., Lawrence Metcalf, and Michael Washburn (1977). "The Crisis of Global Transformation, Interdependence, and the Schools." In B. Frank Brown, Education for Responsible Citizenship. New York: McGraw-Hill.

Meyer, LeAnn (1979). The Citizenship Education Issue: Problems and Programs. Denver: Education Commission of the States.

Mitsakos, Charles L. (1978). "A Global Education Program Can Make A Difference." Theory and Research in Social Education 6, no. 1 (March), pp. 1-15.

Morrissett, Irving, and John D. Haas (1982). "Rationale, Goals, and Objectives in Social Studies." In The Current State of Social Studies: A Report of Project SPAN. Boulder, Colo.: Social Science Education Consortium.

NAEP (1975). "Lay and Subject Matter Reviews of National Assessment Basic Skills Objectives, June 18 to June 25, 1975." Unpublished paper. Denver: National Assessment of Educational Progress.

NAEP (1978). Changes in Social Studies Performance, 1972-76. Denver: National Assessment of Educational Progress.

National Commission on the Reform of Secondary Education (1973). The Reform of Secondary Education. New York: McGraw-Hill.

National Council for the Social Studies (1975). "Social Studies and Its Career Implications." In Garth L. Mangum et al., eds., Career Education in the Academic Classroom. Salt Lake City: Olympus.

National Task Force for High School Reform (1975). The Adolescent, Other Citizens, and Their High Schools. New York: McGraw-Hill.

Newmann, Fred M. (1980). "Political Participation: An Analytic Review and Proposal." In Judith Gillespie and Derek Heater, eds., Political Education in Flux. London: Sage.

Newmann, Fred M. (1975). Education for Citizen Action: Challenge for Secondary Curriculum. Berkeley: McCutchan.

Oliver, Donald W., and James P. Shaver (1966). Teaching Public Issues in the High School. Boston: Houghton Mifflin.

Panel on Youth, President's Science Advisory Committee (1974). Youth: Transition to Adulthood. Chicago: University of Chicago Press.

Parlee, Mary Brown (1979). "The Friendship Bond: PT's Survey Report on Friendship in America." Psychology Today 13, no. 4 (October 1979), pp. 43-54.

Raths, Louis E., Merrill Harmin, and Sidney B. Simon (1978). Values and Teaching, 2nd ed. Columbus, Ohio: Charles E. Merrill.

Remy, Richard C. (1976). "Making, Judging, and Influencing Decisions: A Focus for Citizen Education." Social Education 40, no. 6 (October), pp. 360-365.

Remy, Richard C. (1978a). Consumer and Citizenship Education Today: A Comparative Analysis of Key Assumptions. Columbus, Ohio: Mershon Center, Ohio State University.

Remy, Richard C. (1978b). "Social Studies and Citizenship Education: Elements of a Changing Relationship." Theory and Research in Social Education 6, no. 4 (December), pp. 40-59.

Rose, Caroline B. (1965). <u>Sociology: The Study of Man in Society</u>. Columbus, Ohio: Charles E. Merrill.

Schneider, Donald O. (1980). "Tradition and Change in the Social Studies Curriculum." <u>Journal of Research and Development in Education</u> 13, no. 2 (Winter), pp. 12-23.

Selman, Robert L., and Anne P. Selman (1979). "Children's Ideas About Friendship: A New Theory." <u>Psychology Today</u> 13, no. 4 (October), pp. 71-80, 114.

"Sex Rated Below Friends, School, and Sports" (1979). <u>Denver Post</u>, October 2.

Shaver, James P. (1977). "The Task of Rationale-Building for Citizenship Education." In James P. Shaver, ed., <u>Building Rationales for Citizenship Education</u>. Arlington, Va.: National Council for the Social Studies.

Shaver, James P. (1979). "The Usefulness of Educational Research in Curricular/Instructional Decision Making in Social Studies." <u>Theory and Research in Social Education</u> 7, no. 3 (Fall), pp. 21-46.

Shaver, James P., O.L. Davis, Jr., and Suzanne W. Helburn (1979). <u>An Interpretive Report on the Status of Pre-Collegiate Social Studies Education Based on Three NSF-Funded Studies</u>. Washington, D.C.: National Science Foundation.

Stake, Robert E., and Jack A. Easley, Jr. (1978). <u>Case Studies in Science Education</u>. Washington, D.C.: National Science Foundation.

Stratemeyer, Florence B., et al. (1947). <u>Developing a Curriculum for Modern Living</u>. New York: Teachers College Press.

Tanner, Daniel, and Laurel N. Tanner (1975). <u>Curriculum Development: Theory Into Practice</u>. New York: Macmillan.

Taylor, Bob L., et al. (1977). <u>Tips for Infusing Career Education in the Curriculum</u>. Boulder, Colo.: Social Science Education Consortium.

Torney, Judith V. (1978). "The Elementary School Years as an Optimal Period for Learning About International Human Rights." Paper presented at American Bar Association symposium on Law and the Humanities: Implications for Elementary Education, Chicago.

Torney-Purta, Judith V. (1980). "Recent Psychological Research Relating to Children's Social Cognition and Its Implications for Social and Political Education." In Irving Morrissett and Ann M. Williams, eds., <u>Social/Political Education in Three Countries</u>. Boulder, Colo.: ERIC Clearinghouse for Social Studies/Social Science Education and Social Science Education Consortium, Inc.

Turner, Mary Jane (1980). <u>Developing Your Child's Citizenship Compe-</u>
<u>tence</u>. Boulder, Colo.: Social Science Education Consortium; Mer-
shon Center, Ohio State University.

Walberg, Herbert J., Diane Schiller, and Geneva D. Haertel (1979). "The
Quiet Revolution in Educational Research." <u>Phi Delta Kappan</u> 61,
no. 3 (November), pp. 179-183.

Weiss, Iris R. (1978). <u>National Survey of Science, Mathematics, and</u>
<u>Social Studies Education</u>. Washington, D.C.: National Science
Foundation.

Wiley, Karen B. (1977). <u>The Status of Pre-College Science, Mathematics,</u>
<u>and Social Science Education: 1955-1975</u>, vol. 3. Washington, D.C.:
National Science Foundation.

Wright, David P. (1979). "Social Studies in 38 Schools: Research Findings From a Study of Schooling." Paper presented at the annual
meeting of the National Council for the Social Studies, Portland,
Ore.

Wright, David P. (1980). Correspondence with Project SPAN staff, May/-
June.